MEDICAL NEGLIGENCE: COMPLAINTS AND COMPENSATION

For Sarah and Eileen

Medical Negligence: Complaints and Compensation

JOHN CARRIER
London School of Economics

IAN KENDALL
Portsmouth Polytechnic

Published in Association with
The London School of Economics and Political Science

SERIES EDITOR: JANE LEWIS

Avebury

Aldershot · Brookfield USA · Hong Kong · Singapore · Sydney

Published by
Avebury
Gower Publishing Company Limited
Gower House
Croft Road
Aldershot
Hants GU11 3HR
England

Gower Publishing Company
Old Post Road,
Brookfield
Vermont 05036
USA

ISBN 1 85628 064 0

Printed and Bound in Great Britain by
Athenaeum Press Ltd., Newcastle upon Tyne.

Contents

Acknowledgements vi

List of tables and figures viii

Preface ix

1 Medical negligence, the law and social policy 1

2 The hazards of litigation :
  the role of courts and torts 14

3 Outside the courts :
  state intervention in medicine and health care 32

4 Changes, criteria and conclusions 54

5 Agendas for reform 68

Bibliography 88

Index 94

Acknowledgements

We were helped in the preparation of this book by a number of people.

Its foundations were papers we presented at seminars organised by the Social Administration Association at Cambridge, and the Social Science Research Council at Oxford(1). We would like to thank the organisers of and the participants in those seminars for focusing and developing our interest in this subject. Thanks must also go to those who subsequently read and commented on those papers following the seminar discussions, especially Jeffrey Jowell and Ian Dennis.

A further acknowledgement must go to Michael Ashley-Miller, Max Lehmann and the Nuffield Provincial Hospitals Trust for encouraging us to complete our work on this topic by providing us with the opportunity to present our ideas to a specialist audience in this field at a whole-day seminar in March 1988 (2). The discussion on the outline of this book was most helpful in the preparation of this final version, and while not agreeing with all the points of view expressed, we were nevertheless helped towards an understanding of the implications of our account of the issues for policy reforms.

The final note of thanks must go to Brian Abel-Smith and Joe Jacobs. Both read and commented on our final draft. Of course it remains for us to state that despite the many thought-provoking comments we have received since we began work on this project, the contents, and any errors contained therein remain our responsibility. Hopefully this book will act as a further step towards the understanding of the issues in this complicated field and will engage the attention and interests of lawyers, doctors, social administrators, health service managers and others responsible for redressing the situations that go wrong for the patient.

John Carrier
Ian Kendall
December 1989

(1)Annual Conference of the Social Administration Association on Law and Social Policy,University of Cambridge.1979; and Social Science Research Council on Tort in Relation to Personal Injury and Social Policy,University of Oxford,1980.

(2)Nuffield Provincial Hospitals Trust,Seminar,Doctors,Patients and Medical Negligence,March 1988 - The participants were : Dr.M.Ashley-Miller, Sir Cecil Clothier, Dr.Robert Dingwall, John Finch, Dr.John Fry, Mr.Donald Harris, Anthony Johnson, Dr.John Ledingham, Derek Prentice, Dr.John Wall, Sir Edgar Williams (Chairman).

List of tables and figures

Table 2.1   Highest awards in medical negligence claims
            in the UK   29

Table 3.1   Composition of the GMC before and after the
            Medical Act, 1978   33

Table 3.2   Determinations of the Professional Conduct
            Committee   36

Table 3.3   Analysis of cases dealt with by the GMC   37

Table 4.1   Categories of complaint received by MHAC   63

Figure 2.1 Key stages in taking a case of medical
            negligence through the courts   16

Figure 3.1 Procedures for dealing with complaints
            received by the GMC   35

Figure 3.2 Stages in dealing with clinical complaints
            about the hospital service in the NHS   49

Figure 5.1 Institutions and aims   70

Figure 5.2 Institutions and approaches   72

Figure 5.3 Alternative responses to the consequences
            of disability   81

Preface

The subject-matter of this book is not new. The court's
dealings with questions of medical negligence has been the
subject of several analyses and evaluations from Grunfeld
(1954) to Giesen (1988). In addition there have been
complementary analyses and evaluations of the procedures for
dealing with complaints within the National Health Service such
as Stacey (1965) and Klein (1973). In Klein's case this was
combined with an evaluation of the work of the General Medical
Council. Recently, this has been complemented by Rosenthal's
work on the United Kingdom and Sweden(1987); Quam,Dingwall and
Fenn on the UK and the USA (1987); and Hawkins on the work of
the Medical Defence Union (1985). Despite the attention given
to the subject by a number of previous writers we hope this
book can make an important contribution to the continuing
debate about the most appropriate responses to cases of medical
negligence.

There is a need to up-date some of these earlier analyses in
the light of subsequent developments. But of equal significance
is the need to undertake an analysis of medical negligence in
a form which seeks to combine both administrative and legal
issues. This is an enterprise that is less often undertaken
[another recent example is Jacob (1988)]; one reason may be
that it requires a study that crosses traditional disciplinary
divisions between social and public administration on the one
hand and law on the other. However this disciplinary division
is of little significance to either patients or their doctors,
and we consider the issues involved to be of sufficient
importance to justify our attempt to break out of these
traditional disciplinary confines.

Of course specialist texts on particular procedures for

dealing with complaints about medical care (the courts or the General Medical Council) are an essential precondition for undertaking the more general sort of evaluation we have attempted in this paper. However we would argue that the advantages and disadvantages of particular procedures can be more clearly perceived when they are examined together, rather than in isolation from one another. Furthermore both the necessity and possibilities of change will become clearer when the broader picture is presented. We have written this book in the hope that it will contribute to a broader and clearer picture of how procedures in the UK do and should respond to cases of medical negligence.

The safety of the people requireth...that justice be equally administered to all degrees of people; that is, that as well as the rich and mighty, as poor and obscure persons may be righted of the injuries done to them

Thomas Hobbes, Leviathan, 1651 (1962 edition, pp.302 Fontana)

1 Medical negligence, the law and social policy

The aim of this chapter is to introduce the concept of medical negligence; to explain why it provides the focus for this book and to examine its legal definition in judicial proceedings. We also place the discussion of medical negligence in three broader contexts; the relationships between law and social policy; the relationships between doctors, patients and the state; and some of the ethical issues posed by modern medical practice.

Why medical negligence?

Cases of medical negligence may justifiably be interpreted as merely a proxy and dramatic although unrepresentative tip of a 'submerged iceberg' of friction and grumbles about the NHS (Klein, 1973, DHSS, 1973); they are also only part of a more substantial body of events that might be labelled medical accidents. Is it appropriate in these circumstances to focus on medical negligence?

Cases of 'medical negligence' arise from a diffuse and diverse set of circumstances. They can be placed at one end of a continuum; at the other end is found an enormous volume of relatively minor grumbles and grievances which do not become the subject of legal dispute. We would argue that by addressing the issue of medical negligence we are dealing with some of the most difficult problems that arise from complaints within modern medicine. Medical negligence may provide a good test of the efficiency and fairness of procedures for dealing with all

1

complaints about medical services.

Of course it can be argued that the very seriousness of alleged cases of medical negligence require separate procedures from those designed to deal with less important complaints. We would not dispute this point, but would suggest that it is not possible to place certain events in a precisely labelled category called 'medical negligence' and to set them quite clearly apart from the less serious and less dramatic complaints about medical matters. We may require separate institutions to resolve the more serious and the less serious complaints, but there is a case for linking these institutions. The focus on medical negligence is not only an attempt to seek out better responses to the most serious cases, but also to consider the effectiveness of all the institutions for dealing with complaints about medical matters.

With regard to medical accidents there are both similar and different arguments. Anything less than a comprehensive reform of all social security programmes for physically disabled people, will still leave some individuals having to grapple with the sort of questions of causation and loss that have constituted key elements in legal responses to medical negligence. The area of medical negligence once again exemplifies some of the more difficult questions that have to be resolved. In addition, unlike the broader body of complaints about health care, there are limited alternatives available to the victim of a medical accident. Most of the patients who sue because of a medical accident 'will do so under the law of negligence...the principles underpinning this system and its strengths and weaknesses are, therefore, central to any discussion of the future of compensation for the victims of medical accidents' (Carson,1988,p.1)

Last but not least we must note the significance of medical negligence as an issue in its own right and not simply as part of the broader contexts of complaints about health care and compensation for victims of medical accidents. Questions of professional competence and professional standards are clearly crucial to the quality of health services.

The focus on medical negligence therefore enables us to examine an area where three related and important questions come together.

How do we ensure and maintain the good standards of professional practice which are so important to the quality of modern health care?

How do we ensure adequate compensation for those who suffer losses as a result of the workings of modern health care systems - the victims of accidents and the victims of negligence; those who are bearing part of the costs of other people's progress?

How do we ensure adequate opportunities for individuals to voice their complaints about modern health care systems and obtain adequate redress for those whose complaints are found to be justified?

Our assumption is that these questions should not be addressed in isolation from one another. Thus in finding a 'better answer' to one of them we may contribute to 'better answers' to the others. Our focus on medical negligence is intended to keep all three questions in view.

What is medical negligence?

The law does not define medical or professional negligence as a form of conduct that should be set apart from the conduct of any other member of society offering a service. In the strict legal sense no distinction is drawn between the negligence of a doctor, plumber or window-cleaner. The concept rests entirely on the existence of a duty of care which is owed by all individuals in society to all other individuals, as illustrated by the following legal definitions.

> Negligence...is the omission to do something which a reasonable man guided by those considerations which ordinarily regulate the conduct of human affairs, would do; or doing something which a prudent and reasonable man would not do. (Blyth v Birmingham Waterworks Co,,1856,11 Ex.781, Baron Alderson)

> The liability for negligence..is no doubt based upon a general public sentiment of moral wrongdoing for which the offender must pay. But acts or omissions which any moral code would censure cannot in a practical world be treated so as to give a right to every person injured by them to demand relief...the rule that you are to love your neighbour becomes in law, you must not injure your neighbour...(for the purposes of law your neighbour is)...persons who are so closely and directly affected by my act that I ought reasonably to have them in contemplation as being so affected when I am directing my mind to the acts or omissions which are called into question. (Donoghue v Stevenson,1932,A.C.562, 1932 S.C. (H.L.)31, Lord Atkin)

This general concept of negligence is closely related to its specific use in cases of medical negligence. There is obviously an expectation that the professional person will be able to exercise more skill than the lay person.

> Where you get a situation which involves the use of some special skill or competence, then the test as to whether there has been negligence or not is not the test of the man on top of a Clapham omnibus, because he has not got this special skill.

However continuing his judgement in that case, McNair J also stated that:

> the test is the standard of the ordinary skilled man exercising and professing to have that special skill...a

3

man need not possess the highest expert skill; it is well established law that it is sufficient if he exercises the ordinary skill of an ordinary competent man exercising that particular art. (<u>Bolam v Friern Barnet Hospital Management Committee</u>,1957,1 W.L.R.582.586)

The standard of care that is used to establish negligence is therefore that of the average practitioner of the class to which the defendant belongs, this being neither a very high nor a very low standard, but a fair and reasonable standard of skill and competence. Over sixty years ago this civil liability of medical practitioners towards their patients was stated as follows:

> If a person holds himself out as possessing special skills and knowledge and he is consulted, as possessing such skill and knowledge, by or on behalf of a patient, he owes a duty to the patient to use due caution in undertaking the treatment. If he accepts the responsibility and undertakes the treatment and the patient submits to his direction and treatment accordingly, he owes a duty to the patient to use diligence, care, knowledge, skill and caution in administering the treatment. No contractual relationship is necessary nor is it necessary that the service be rendered for reward....the law requires a fair and reasonable standard of care and competence. The standard must be reached in all matters above mentioned. If the patient's death has been caused by the defendant's indolence or carelessness it will not avail to show that he had sufficient knowledge; nor will it avail to prove that he was diligent in attendance, if the patient has been killed by his gross ignorance and unskilfulness. (<u>R v Bateman</u>,1925,94 LJKB,791)

It is accepted that some practitioners will show greater skill than others, but:

> the true test for establishing negligence in diagnosis or treatment on the part of a doctor is whether he has been proved guilty of such failure as no doctor of ordinary skill would be guilty of, if acting with reasonable care. (<u>Hunter v Hanley</u>,1955,SLT 213)

Thus in the same way as the courts are concerned generally with what the prudent person would or would not have done, the exercise by a physician of his or her professional function operates in itself to impose a legal duty of care: that of an ordinarily skilled physician in the relevant speciality (Giesen,1988,p.xiv).
This duty may be said to derive from the fact that the

> practitioner does something to a human being which is likely to cause physical damage unless it is done with proper care and skill. It is well settled that under those circumstances the practitioner owes a duty in tort to the patient. (Percy,1977,p.579)

4

Once again this can be linked to general principles applicable to all cases of negligence.

> a man who traverses a crowded thoroughfare with edged tools or bars of iron, must take especial care that he does not cut or bruise with the things he carries. (<u>Franklin v Bristol Tramways & Carriage Co Ltd</u>,1941,1KB 255)

As applied to medical practice it may be said that 'a prudent man handles a scalpel with greater care than a magnifying glass' (Martin,1973,p.363).

It would be inappropriate to accept these legal definitions of medical negligence in an uncritical manner and we identify some of the problems in Chapter Two. However they clearly have much to commend them. It would be unrealistic to expect all medical practitioners to provide a standard of care which is available from the most skilled and able of their profession. We may wish to narrow the gap between the average and the best practitioners, and it may be possible to pursue a number of policies towards that end; but at the same time it would be unrealistic to assume the existence of a large professional group all of whom are practising medicine at a virtually identical and very high standard.

The legal definitions of negligence allow for standards to be set that are appropriate to current circumstances. These standards can and do change with changes in medicine. But the legal definition remains as an enduring working principle. This is partly because professional negligence does not refer to some special form of conduct that is only expected of professional persons, but is rooted in the legal obligations of all members of society to one another. It is also because it does not refer to the exceptional work of the very best practitioner working at the frontiers of current medical knowledge, but to the normal prudent work of the average practitioner utilising well-established medical practices.

Whatever its merits, the courts have not found it easy to apply this concept of medical negligence. Deciding what an average medical practitioner would do in any one set of circumstances is not a straightforward task, and depends on the current state of knowledge, training, motivation and peer-review. One dilemma which is not readily resolved is how to reconcile the desirable aim of eliminating 'bad practice' (and the 'bad practitioner') with the need to arrive at a fair and workable definition of what might be said to constitute 'bad practice' (see Chapter Two).

Law and welfare

The relationship between law and welfare can be said to embrace three main categories. They are as follows:

Welfare through the law (judicial welfare)

Welfare law

Law as welfare

Welfare through the law (or judicial welfare) concerns the role of 'redistribution by the courts' in meeting needs in modern industrial societies. It is generally accepted that state welfare activities include both conventional social welfare programmes - eg the NHS - and aspects of the tax system (fiscal welfare) (Titmuss,1963,Ch.2). The welfare role of the courts has been given less recognition, but there is clearly a case for regarding the courts as another dimension of state welfare activities (Titmuss,1974,Ch.6).

Of particular interest is the extent to which the courts can effectively and equitably compensate groups and individuals for the social costs and disservices generated by a complex, changing society, for example with regard to compensation for personal injury resulting from negligent acts. A common theme of much writing on this issue concerns the limitations of judicial institutions and procedures for dealing with a number of social problems (eg mental illness, see Jones,1960,p.10 and Roberts,1967,p.13; race relations, see Little,1977). However it would be misleading to assume that arguments on welfare issues are always in favour of conventional social welfare programmes and against the use of judicial welfare. Concern was expressed about the operation of the Children and Young Persons Act,1969 and the Mental Health Act,1959 in terms of the insufficient protection afforded to the rights of the individuals by legislation which sought to diminish significantly the role of conventional judicial institutions and procedures (see, for example, Morris et al, 1980, and Gostin, 1975). 'Welfare' considerations will therefore not lead us to assume automatically that there is no role for judicial welfare in responding to cases of medical negligence - although as we shall see the role of the courts in these cases raises all the usual questions about the appropriateness of court proceedings as a response to the problem and the needs of those affected (see Chapter Two).

Welfare law concerns the nature of the laws upon which conventional social welfare programmes are based. This includes such issues as the extent to which statutes confer rights to welfare on citizens, as opposed to discretionary powers on welfare agencies and welfare personnel (see,Davis,1971). The concept of a 'right to welfare' is not easily translated into effective practice - most notably with services in kind, where it is difficult to state with any precision what should be the duties of the welfare agencies (eg the NHS) or the rights of welfare service users (eg NHS patients). The 'right to complain' can be seen as an important adjunct to the 'right to welfare', since an independent complaints machinery might be expected to provide guidance on rights and duties. How effectively such machinery can fulfil this, and other broader roles, is an issue that arises in any analysis of the procedures for dealing with medical negligence. Our ideas about medical negligence must also be related to our ideas about the duties of medical professionals, the use of their often considerable discretionary powers, and the rights of their patients, including their 'right to know'.

Law as welfare concerns the provision of legal services to citizens and the extent to which such provision should be considered a legitimate dimension of state welfare activities. In Britain official acceptance of the idea of 'legal services' as a part of state welfare could be said to date from the passing of the Legal Aid and Advice Act in 1949.

These three categories of the law and welfare are obviously related. The scope of publicly provided legal services (law as welfare) will influence the ease or difficulty with which an individual citizen might pursue a matter (such as a case of medical negligence) through the courts (judicial welfare). Welfare law may make provision for specialist 'welfare tribunals' to deal with issues (such as complaints about the NHS). Once again the provision of legal services (law as welfare) may be an important determinant of how effectively the consumer can use such tribunals. Welfare laws may also embody certain ideas about consumer/citizen rights and public representation and participation, and procedures for controlling the quality of services. All of these may have an important bearing on the incidence of, and responses to, cases of medical negligence.

Doctors, patients and the state

The development of the National Health Service (NHS) since 1948 may be analysed in terms of the relationship between the medical profession, the service user (or patient), and the state. Many of the standard texts on the NHS place considerable emphasis on the concept of professionalism. That is the idea that professional power and influence have been, and remain key determinants of both the historical development and current working of the NHS - that for example, the organization of the NHS represents 'a victory of tactical considerations over administrative logic and coherence' (Klein,1983,p.x; see also Eckstein,1959; Willcocks,1967; Allsop,1984; and Ham,1985).

For the individual professional however, whether general practitioner or hospital consultant, the concepts of professional power and influence may seem increasingly outmoded. The tradition associated with independent professional practice and clinical autonomy may appear to the practitioners themselves to have been steadily eroded and increasingly circumscribed in two respects. Firstly, there is a critical, yet highly expectant, body of consumers and client-orientated pressure groups (see, for example, Kennedy,1981). Secondly, there is central government's increasing interest and activity in setting priorities and allocating resources within the NHS especially since the publication of the priorities documents and more recently the report of the Management Inquiry Team (Griffiths Report, 1983) and its implication for clinical budgeting. Studies of patient complaints, medical error and negligence, and methods of administrative and legal redress, might be seen as yet a further indication by a beleaguered medical profession of them coming under scrutiny in yet another area of professional life in which the rest of the community have unjustifiably high expectations of their competence (see, Jacob,1988,p.55-56).

From the perspective of the individual patient, it is unlikely that the prestige and the autonomy associated with the professional practice of medicine will be seen as a thing of the past. This lay perspective is supportable by those official statistics and surveys that suggest that while relatively few NHS patients have complaints about the service they receive (see, Merrison Report, 1979, para.11.12), there appears to be a 'submerged iceberg' of friction and grumbles which go unrecorded in the official figures (Klein, 1973, DHSS, 1973). Without a large-scale research programme it is not possible to know whether professional prestige acts as a deterrent to these potential complainants. Those whose complaints do form part of the official statistics may well testify to the continuing significance of professional autonomy in the limitations placed on the scope of inquiry and jurisdiction of the Health Service Commissioner (see, Chapter Four). Professional power and influence may also be interpreted as factors in explaining the delays in reforming the complaints machinery for general practitioner services (see,Chapter Three).

For central government the medical profession has been seen as both a powerful ally and an implacable foe. Both Enoch Powell and Richard Crossman (a previous Minister of Health and Secretary of State for Social Services respectively) found the medical profession to be influential in deciding what happens in the NHS (Powell,1966; Crossman,1972). Central government's interest in setting priorities and allocating resources since the mid 1970s may signify an attempt to reduce and control professional influence on such matters. But the available evidence shows that this has not proved easy to put into practice. The public expenditure restraints of the 1970s and 1980s will have been partially responsible for the problems faced by the Health Service. But professional opposition to some of the priorities of central government, and the resulting allocations which have flowed from these priorities, have also have played their part in producing a climate of opinion within the health service of uncertainty, conflict, professional dissatisfaction and distrust of what are interpreted as purely 'political' decisions.

It seems likely that one's view of the nature and significance of professionalism will vary according to one's position in the system of nationalised health care, whether as patient, doctor or representative of the state. On the other hand there is almost certainly a degree of consensus about the desirability of sustaining standards of professional competence that ensure the effective and ethical application of medical expertise. At this general level all will be against medical negligence. But there may of course be considerable disagreement on procedures for prevention, investigation, and compensation. Such disagreements may partly reflect different interests, but they may also reflect the complexities of the ethical issues involved in the delivery of medical care in modern systems of health care (see,for example, Downie and Calman,1987, and Mason and McCall Smith,1983).

Ethical issues

Medical negligence is an example of where three sets of valued goals come together. These are firstly, unlimited access to knowledge through educational institutions because medicine is widely perceived as a knowledge-based, scientific enterprise; secondly, the promotion of individual health through access to medical care institutions because public expectations are that medical care should do no harm, even if through personal circumstances (eg genetic endowment) it is unable to restore the individual to functional health status; and thirdly, the guarantee of justice through access to legal institutions based on the public expectation that only the judiciary can redress wrongs done to lay-people by professionals because the judiciary work from a body of recorded case-law and precedent, thereby giving what Hart calls the 'rule of recognition' by which decisions can be legitimised.

We should begin by briefly reminding ourselves of some of the more obvious ethical dilemmas posed by the provision of medical care to individuals and for the community as a whole. For doctors, three particularly significant ethical issues are those relating to questions of resources, research, and relationships.

Firstly, there is the question of how disputes over the allocation of resources are resolved. These disputes involve, for example, how to resolve the conflict between drives for efficiency in the health system, and the doctors' concern to protect the individuality of the patient. This is the often reported drama of shortage of resources for technologically dependent, life-threatened patients (e.g.hole-in-the heart babies), who face competing demands from less life threatening, but low quality of life, patients (see, for example, Jacob,1988,p.59).

The second issue concerns research. Disputes over persons who are dependent being in experiments for the greater good of patients to come, set against the autonomy of the individual in the trial (see, for example, the American trial of Interluken 2,Horizon,BBC-2, 29 February 1988, see also the case in New Zealand (Cartwright Report,1988) and that of Mrs.Evelyn Thomas, see, The Observer,9 & 16 October,1988).

The third issue is that of interpersonal professional/lay relationships. Although the dramatic questions of sexual deviance, drink, and drugs usually dominate this area, the related questions of confidentiality and trust in the professional are raised by such issues (see, for example, Kennedy,1987). In the end the question is whether the professional's judgement has been, or could be impaired ?

The significance of such issues - resources, research and relationships - force us to consider the ethical underpinning of the profession's right to self-regulation. As we have already indicated, recent trends may appear to be pulling the profession in different directions in terms of the traditional professional claim to be given the discretion to apply their knowledge in a therapeutically effective and ethically acceptable manner. 'Consumerist' concerns with the patient's right to know may seek to remove the resolution of ethical

9

dilemmas from the province of the professional and transfer it to the patient. 'Managerial' concerns with clinical budgeting may force professionals to continue to resolve ethical dilemmas within a fixed resource framework - thus relieving others (especially managers and politicians) of the need to address these issues.

There have always been radically opposed views on the appropriateness of professional self-regulation. For Adam Smith, 'people of the same trade seldom meet together, even for merriment and diversion, but the conversation ends in a conspiracy against the public or in some contrivance to raise prices' (Adam Smith, 1776). This observation was echoed in George Bernard Shaw's subsequent assertion that all the professions were a 'conspiracy against the laity'. Alternatively, the conduct of doctors towards their patients may be regarded as largely determined by

> feelings of professional responsibility and awareness of ethical considerations .... the well-being of the patient ... (transcending) any thought of financial advantage, convenience or professional advancement. (Knight, 1982, p.4)

Medical ethics involves the duties of medical persons to the public, to each other and to themselves in regard to the exercise of their profession; they require us to think about a balance between public regulation, professional rules and private conscience. The Adam Smith and Shavian view leads to a mistrust of the self-regulation of professional rules and private conscience as sufficient restraints on professional activity. The emphasis may be on public regulation and the need to encase the medical profession in a web of political, bureaucratic and judicial controls, or alternatively on exposing professional conduct to the invigorating and cleansing blast of free market forces. Other views would place more faith in the profession's ability to manage its own affairs and to ensure that whatever controls are established allow adequate scope for professional autonomy - including the application of professional knowledge guided by professional ethics.

Some of the dilemmas in this area therefore reflect our willingness or unwillingness to trust the professions. As we suggested earlier, different views may well reflect one's position in the 'health care system'. Patients are probably more willing to place their trust in the professionals, rather than in the managers and the politicians, on issues of resources; but may well be coming less trusting in areas of research, and more anxious to be fully involved in decisions about their own medical care. Managers and politicians are not willing to trust the profession to exercise its autonomy on resource issues, but are equally unwilling to face up to the ethical dilemmas posed by the restraints they set on resources. Given the complex and profound nature of some of these ethical dilemmas, the question arises of whether we can develop systems of control and compensation that provide more effective opportunities for the resolution of these issues ?

What any system of control or compensation also has to come to terms with are the differing expectations about the values which might inform medical decision-making. These include:

a deontological approach which emphasises a rigid code of duties which should be acted on at all times by doctors;

the categorical imperative which emphasises individual autonomy, impartiality and respect for others; and

a utilitarian approach which emphasises the benefits or costs to the wider community

The reality may be that in the end the professionals find their decisions are underpinned by a shifting combination of these (and other) ethical approaches. Thus utilitarian considerations may be virtually absent in decisions about forms of treatment whose efficacy has been clearly demonstrated and whose costs are negligible. But in committing substantial resources to new, and as yet unproven, treatments on the current 'frontiers of medical science' it may be difficult to avoid the ethics of utilitarianism. Indeed when we look at the oldest remedy for complaints about doctors (the courts), it is interesting to examine the content of judicial decision-making and see the way in which different ethical approaches are combined. For example, there has been a presumption that patients must accept the risks inherent in medical practice, at least in part for utilitarian reasons - that the community at large stands to benefit from medical advances, and medical advances involve experimentation which involves risks (see, Chapter Two).

This ethical plurality is often utilised in four distinct areas whereby 'knowledgeable' doctors face 'unknowledgeable' patients. These are questions of consent, choice, compliance and contract.

Consent

English law does not recognise a doctrine of 'informed consent' (see, Chapter Two), but most medical procedures carried out on patients are assumed to be based upon consent and therefore the doctors are not in the position of assaulting the person or integrity of the patient.

Choice

Although the assumption that patients have a choice in the type of treatment and the medical practitioner they wish to treat them, the reality of unequal knowledge between patient and doctor, scarce resources, and sometimes uncertain outcomes from medical procedures, means that choice can rarely approximate to the true meaning of an informed decision based upon full knowledge of consequences, thus acting as a protection to doctors 'when things go wrong'.

Compliance

There is an assumption, following the ideas of consent and choice, that all patients comply with professional decisions about treatment and advice. Again however in the real world this is unlikely to be the case. The authoritative position of the doctor may compel compliance with the treatment; and any deviation from compliance leaves the blame for an unsuccessful outcome firmly with the patient, whereas an unsuccessful outcome following full patient compliance may still leave the doctor protected on the basis of current medical knowledge (for an interesting discussion of these issues, see, Jacob, 1988, Ch.6, esp.p.169).

Contract

There is an assumed contract existing between the doctor and the patient. If this were to be challenged it might mean the replacing of a duty of care with a duty of competence, for a number of reasons. Firstly, the concept of care has psychological meaning, as against a purely physical activity directed at the patient for a defined condition by a doctor's advice or intervention. The assumption is that such an intervention can remedy or reduce a pathological condition with a return to an assumed normality. Secondly, this itself raises the 'standard of care' issue and whether or not it is reasonable to expect 'the average practitioner' to aspire to the standard of 'the exceptional practitioner'. Thirdly, the nature of the contract, especially for general practitioners (24 hours a day, 7 days a week, see S.I 1974/160, paras 13,14), raises the question of the extent to which an average practitioner can be responsible for the standard of his employed surrogate carer (locum, deputy, see S.I.1982/1283, para 7b)? Is it reasonable for the practitioner to be responsible for the quality of the surrogate? Should the surrogate's inability to enforce patient compliance be a responsibility of the general practitioner? This may also occur in the situation where a consultant psychiatrist discharges a patient into the community, but is unable to guarantee compliance with a drug stabilisation programme.

Which ethic - the professional ethic of duty, the personal ethic of the categorical imperative, or the workplace ethic of utilitarianism should structure the behaviour of doctors? How should the system of redress reflect the ethical frameworks that implicitly guide doctors decisions in these areas?

Conclusions

It will be seen that our seemingly narrow focus on the example of medical negligence requires consideration of questions that impinge on a number of dimensions of the relationship between law and welfare, on many aspects of the organization and administration of health services, on the broader issue of professional negligence within state welfare, and on the ethical issues that arise. We should also remember that cases of medical negligence may have a most profound impact on certain patients, their families and friends. They may also be of considerable significance for the lives of the professional people involved. With these considerations in mind we will begin our examination of the various procedures through which patients may seek redress against practitioners whom they claim have been negligent, and through which the practitioner may seek to defend themselves against such claims.

The organising principle of the next three chapters is basically chronological. The oldest remedies were the courts of law (see, Chapter Two) and the disciplinary powers of the Royal College of Physicians, the College of Surgeons and the Apothecaries Society. The latter were succeeded by the establishment of what has become the General Medical Council following the Medical Act, 1858; state involvement in National Health Insurance and then the National Health Service introduced further avenues through which patients grievances could be aired (see, Chapter Three). We conclude with an examination of the range of relatively new institutions concerned with the maintenance of good standards of medical care and judging complaints about the failure to achieve these standards (see, Chapter Four).

2 The hazards of litigation: the role of courts and torts

Soldiers finde warres, and lawyers finde out still
Litigious men, which quarrels move.
    John Donne, The Canonization, Early Seventeenth Century

I practice the law, I am not only willing but anxious to
sue anyone, anytime.
    Mr.Johnson the lawyer in the film 'The Miracle of
    Morgans Creek' (1944)

Most people in Britain currently receive most of their health
care through the National Health Service. If we feel aggrieved
about the quality of care we may think firstly in terms of
complaining about the NHS, and as we shall see systems for
dealing with such complaints have evolved with the extension of
state intervention in health care (see, Chapters 3 and 4). But
avenues of complaint were available to aggrieved patients
before there was extensive state provision of health services.
One such avenue was itself the result of specific state
intervention. This was the Medical Act of 1858 through which
what we now know as the General Medical Council acquired
disciplinary powers over members of the medical profession
(see,Chapter 3). The other avenue was the oldest, and for a
long time the most important, method of obtaining compensation
for personal injury. This is civil liability in tort which
covers wrongful acts and omission, other than breaches of
contract, in respect of which damages can be claimed by the
victim from the wrong-doer for loss or injury.
    The historical roots of civil liability in tort lie in the
tradition of paying a forfeit for harm done. This tradition was
also found in other European systems and rested upon no clear
distinction between crime and tort. Subsequently, serious crime

came to be punishable by the state rather than by private vengeance and vendetta and the exaction of compensation by the injured party or his relatives (see,Pearson Report,1978,Ch.4). However there remained the less serious cases for which the principle of reparation began to be acknowledged by the Common Law, through a developing law of tort. This branch of law had as its major concern compensation, where an individual was injured or property damaged. Pecuniary compensation, or damages, thus became the significant outcome for all parties in a tort action.

By the beginning of the nineteenth century, 'the courts were saying that those who publicly professed an occupation requiring skill should exercise care and knowledge' (Jacob and Davies,1987,p.1-34). The resulting legal concept of negligence as a specific tort consisted of 'a breach of legal ... duty owed by a practitioner or craftsman to exercise care in the practice of his calling' (Martin,1973,p.353). Thus 'the oldest remedy for a patient dissatisfied with the services provided by a doctor is to go to law ... that is he can bring an action for negligence' (Martin,1973,p.353). As we have already noted most of those individuals who sue because of a medical accident do so under the law of negligence (Carson,1988).

We begin our detailed examination of ways of dealing with medical negligence by looking at what we have termed judicial welfare or welfare through the law, which will include the role of the courts in deciding the outcome of actions in tort. Apart from its historical significance, the decisions of the courts on questions of medical negligence have a dramatic effect on the compensation paid to aggrieved patients and to the professional standing of doctors. They have a further impact upon whether or not the state reviews its regulations and laws regarding the operation of the complaints machinery in the NHS. High levels of damages as compensation also have a bearing on the role of social security payments. What may appear to be a 'private affair' between a patient and doctor, often turns out to have an impact beyond the intentions of the complainant, or the actions of the professionals.

Courts and torts

The starting point for an action for negligence could be the County Courts which have jurisdiction to entertain nearly all types of claim which may be the subject of civil proceedings in the High Court. In general, the judge of a county court is the sole judge in all proceedings; the court, on an application made by any party to the proceedings, may allow the trial to be with a jury. However County Courts are limited to those cases where the damage claimed is not more than £5000. For most cases of alleged medical negligence, the case will be heard by the High Court - the divisions of which were reorganised following the Administration of Justice Act,1970. Subsequent appeals are heard by the Court of Appeal and the House of Lords (see, Figure 2.1).

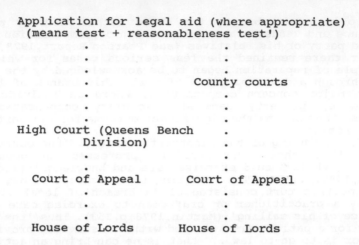

Application for legal aid (where appropriate)
(means test + reasonableness test')

County courts

High Court (Queens Bench
Division)

Court of Appeal   Court of Appeal

House of Lords   House of Lords

Figure 2.1 Key stages in taking a case of medical negligence
through the courts

For many individuals the real starting point may be the legal
aid provisions (law as welfare). Civil proceedings may be
lengthy and costly and few people may be able to entertain an
action without the availability of some assistance from the
state. Legal aid in civil proceedings is available to any
person whose disposable income does not exceed a specified sum
per annum. However, if disposable capital exceeds the specified
sum and it appears the plaintiff can afford to proceed without
it, legal aid may be refused, or may have to be repaid
subsequently for those in certain income bands. As well as this
means test, a person applying for legal aid has to show that
they have reasonable grounds for taking, defending, or being a
party to the proceedings in question. A person may therefore be
refused legal aid on grounds of either means or where it
appears unreasonable that they should receive it.

If one's own resources, or the operation of the legal aid
scheme, do not preclude one from pursuing one's case, on what
basis will the courts decide its merits? In an action for
negligence the plaintiff has to show that the defendant owed
him or her a duty of care, that the defendant in breach of that
duty behaved negligently, and that the defendant's negligent
behaviour caused damage to the plaintiff. In proving his or her
case the onus of proof lies on the plaintiff (<u>Wilsher v Essex
AHA</u>, 1988, W.L.R., 25 March, p.557), but the burden of proof on
the plaintiff is lighter in a civil action than in a criminal
prosecution, in that the plaintiff has only to establish a
balance of probabilities in his or her favour, whereas the
prosecutor in a criminal case has to prove his case beyond
reasonable doubt (see,Pearson Report,1978,p.19-20). However it
may be argued that the burden of proof should be greater in a
case of professional negligence as Lord Denning suggested:

a charge of professional negligence against a medical man
was serious. It stood on a different footing to a charge

16

of negligence against the driver of a car. The consequences
were far more serious. It affected his professional status
and reputation. The burden of proof was correspondingly
greater. As the charge was so grave, so should the proof be
clear. (Cole v Hucks,1968,C.A.,The Times,9 May 1968)

Where liability for negligence is established, damages are
awarded for monetary and non-monetary loss. The main types of
monetary loss are likely to be expenses incurred as a result of
the accident, loss of earnings and loss of future earning
capacity. Classes of non-monetary loss include loss of physical
function, pain and suffering, disfigurement, and loss of
amenity, for example the inability to pursue a particular
leisure activity (see,Civil Justice Review,1988,paras.398-399).
We will use the three elements of an action for negligence –
a duty of care, negligent behaviour and damage to the plaintiff
as a framework within which we can examine some of the problems
the courts have had to resolve, and how they have resolved
them.

(i) The duty owed by the defendant to the plaintiff to exercise
    care

   A man cannot be charged with negligence if he has no duty
   to exercise diligence.
   (Donoghue v Stevenson,1932, AC 562)

The first question is how we can establish whether a
defendant owes a duty to the plaintiff (see,Jacob and Davies,
1987, pp.1-38). Lord Atkin stated the general principle by
saying that the duty was owed to:

   persons who are so closely and directly affected by my act
   that I ought reasonably to have them in contemplation as
   being so affected when I am directing my mind to the acts
   or omissions which are called into question. (Donoghue v
   Stevenson,1932, A.C. 562)

Patients claiming against their own doctors or a hospital
usually have no difficulty in establishing that the defendant
owed them a duty of care (see,Brazier,1987,p.70). What has been
reinterpreted by the courts this century, is whether hospitals
incur liability when they undertake responsibility for a
patient's treatment, and, due to their employees negligence, a
patient suffers injury (see, Giesen, 1988, p.50). The medical
practitioner was and still remains liable. The situation is now
that 'hospitals...are vicariously liable for their employees'
acts and omissions' (Giesen, 1988, p.51). This was not always
the case, and at one time the principle was firmly settled that

   if reasonable care was taken to select competent
   physicians, surgeons and nurses, the hospital authorities
   were not responsible for their negligence in the course
   of their professional duties. (Percy,1977,p.585)

This view was accepted after a series of cases beginning with

<u>Hillyer v St.Barthlomews Hospital</u> (1909) 2 K.B.820 where the plaintiff entered the hospital to be medically examined under an anaesthetic. While the court found that Hillyer was negligently placed on the operating table so that his arms were burnt, bruised and paralysed, it ruled that the Governors were not liable for this negligent act (see,Jacob(ed),1978,p.254).

This principle remained intact until <u>Gold v Essex County Council</u> (1943) 2 All.E.R.237. The lower court held that the hospital authority was not legally liable for the negligent acts of their professional staff, but the Court of Appeal reversed the decision by making a distinction between medical staff on a 'contract for service' (eg consultants) and those employed on a 'contract of service' (eg nursing staff). They ruled that vicarious liability applied in the latter case, but not the former - a difficult principle to apply when both categories of staff work together as a team.

The vicarious responsibility of the hospital was effectively established by the judgement in <u>Cassidy v Minister of Health</u> (1951) 2.K.B. 343. In this case the plaintiff, who was suffering from a contraction of the third and fourth finger, was operated upon by Dr.Fahrni. After the operation, the plaintiff's hand and forearm were bandaged to a splint and they remained so for some fourteen days. During this time the plaintiff complained of pain, but apart from the administration of sedatives no action was taken. When the bandages were removed, it was found that all four fingers of the plaintiff's hand were stiff and that the hand was practically useless. For the defendants it was contended that, assuming that there was negligence, it was either the negligence of the doctor, or it was uncertain who was the negligent party, and in either case the defendants were not responsible. This view of the hospital authority's responsibilities was rejected both in the original judgement and in the Court of Appeal where Lord Denning made the following observations:

> The truth is that, in cases of negligence, the distinction between a contract of service and a contract for services only becomes of importance when it is sought to make the employer liable, not for a breach of his own duty of care, but for some collateral act of negligence by those whom he employs. He cannot escape the consequences of a breach of his own duty.. in the present case... we are not concerned with any collateral or causal acts of negligence by the staff, but negligence in the treatment itself which it was the employer's duty to provide. (All England Law Reports, 3.3.51,pp.587-589)

Subsequent cases confirmed the vicarious liabilities of hospitals, although this principle has itself been deprived of practical significance by the development of a new approach to the liability of hospital authorities. This is the tendency to

> treat the problem of the hospital authority's liability as raising issues of primary as well as vicarious responsibility; the hospital authority is now considered to be under a duty to its patients which it does not

discharge simply by delegating its performance, whether to a servant or an independent contractor. (Giesen, 1988, p.59)

This change should not be seen in isolation from the broader social and political context. It is accepted that the virtual disappearance of the voluntary hospitals with the establishment of the National Health Service influenced the acceptance of the principles of vicarious and direct liability (see,Martin,1973,p.383).

By the same token the administrative and managerial arrangements of the new Service were important. Partly in response to pressure from the medical profession, the general practitioners retained their 'independent contractor' status and hence the authorities responsible for the family practitioner services have not been liable for the torts of these practitioners, unless 'it arises from their active interference in the execution of work by a practitioner' (Martin,1973,p.141).

(ii) What is taken to constitute a breach of the duty of care?

Despite changing circumstances, there are concepts of duty and degrees of care which do not change. For example,

a medical practitioner must attend to his patient with reasonable promptitude ... failure to do this, or an unreasonable delay ... may give rise to a cause of action in damages. (Martin,1973,p.364; see SI 1974/160 para.14)

The duty of care is held to include the exercise of reasonable foresight. What is reasonably foreseeable for the prudent practitioner will be decided in the light of medical knowledge and orthodox practice at the time.

In the case of Roe v Ministry of Health, ampoules containing an anaesthetic developed invisible cracks, through which percolated the phenol in which they had been stored, and as a result, two patients suffered spinal paralysis following injections of the material. The court held that having regard to the state of medical knowledge at the relevant time, the anaesthetist was not negligent in having taken no precautions to guard against such a risk (1954, 2 Q.B.66). Similarly, a surgeon was held not to be liable when he made an incorrect diagnosis through his failure to use an instrument which was very rare in England at the material date (Whiteford v Hunter (1950) W.N.553; see, Percy, 1977, p.580).

The courts have clearly recognised that there is an element of risk in medical practice, and this must be taken into account when assessing medical negligence (see, for example, Marshall v Lindsey County Council (1935) 1 K.B. 516). Indeed Lord Denning's judgment in Roe v Ministry of Health uses the economic model of risk, enterprise, technical innovation and initiative.

Medical science has conferred great benefits on mankind but these benefits are attended by considerable risks.

Every surgical operation is attended by risks. We cannot take the benefits without taking the risks. Every advance in technique is also attended by risks. Doctors, like the rest of us, have to learn by experience; and experience often teaches in a hard way.

He went on to argue that:

> we should be doing a disservice to the community at large if we were to impose liability on hospitals and doctors for everything that happens to go wrong. Doctors would be led to think more of their own safety than of the good of their patients. Initiative would be stifled and confidence shaken. A proper state of proportion requires us to have regard to the conditions in which hospitals and doctors have to work. We must insist on due care for the patient at every point, but we must not condemn as negligence that which is only a misadventure. (<u>Roe v Ministry of Health</u> (1954) A.E.R.,13.5.54, p137 and p.139)

Lord Denning was involved in another case where issues of risk and medical knowledge were in dispute. This was <u>Crawford v Charing Cross Hospital</u> where it was held that an anaesthetist who had failed to read an article in 'The Lancet' describing the risks of the operation, had been negligent. Lord Denning held that:

> it would be putting too high a burden on a medical man to say that he must read every article in the medical press...the medical man's duty is limited to taking reasonable steps to keep himself abreast of modern developments in technique...failure to read a particular article may well be excusable, while disregard for a series of warnings in the medical press would perhaps be cogent evidence of negligence. (1953,T.L.R.; see also, Martin, 1973, p.361)

Lord Denning was given an opportunity to re-emphasise the main principles of these judgements in the case of <u>Whitehouse v Jordan</u>. In this case, the defendant, a senior hospital registrar, was in charge of the delivery of the plaintiff as a baby following a high risk pregnancy. After the mother had been in labour for 22 hours the defendant decided to carry out a test to see whether forceps could be used to assist the delivery. In doing so the defendant followed a suggestion by his head of department, a consultant professor of obstetrics, in his case notes on the mother. The defendant pulled on the baby with the forceps five or six times and then fearing for the safety of the mother and child, he carried out a Caesarean section quickly and competently. The plaintiff was born with severe brain damage and, acting by his father and subsequently his mother, brought an action in negligence against the defendant alleging want of professional skill and care by pulling too hard and too long on the forceps and so causing the brain damage. In his interpretation of an expert witness and the mother's evidence, the judge found that the defendant had pulled too hard and too long on the forceps causing the foetus to become wedged in the birth canal, that in unwedging the foetus he had caused asphyxia which in turn had caused cerebral palsy and that in so using the forceps he fell below the high standard of professional competence required by the law, and was therefore negligent.

The defendant appealed and the appeal was allowed on the grounds that even if the defendant had pulled too hard and too long with the forceps, that was an error of clinical judgement and did not amount to negligence in the legal sense. In addition it was pointed out that expert opinion was divided as to whether in this instance the forceps had been applied for too long and with too much force. Lord Denning commented that in his judgement there is a danger in cases regarding members of the professions 'of their being made liable whenever something happens to go wrong'. With doctors

> if they are to be found liable whenever they do not effect a cure, or whenever anything untoward happen...it would do a great disservice to the profession itself...(and)..not only to the profession but to society at large. (<u>Whitehouse v Jordan & others</u>,1980,1 All E.R.p.658)

How much and what sort of information should be given to the patient? Where there has been a mishap the patient must be told. Where in giving treatment by injection a needle was broken, without negligence, and left in the patient's body, it was held to be negligence not to tell the patient of the presence of the broken needle (<u>Gerber v Pines</u>, 1933, 79 S.J.13, see, Percy, 1977, pp.581-582). But is it negligent for a doctor to withhold information about the risks attached to certain types of treatment? <u>Mullins v Parsons</u> involved two operations for deafness in which a surgeon inserted an electronic device under the skin near to the left ear. The second operation was to remove it, but the surgeon admitted he had left 'in situ' gold wires covered with plastic. The patient experienced facial paralysis and other injuries, liability for which was admitted. The trial judge said that he was satisfied that if the patient had been warned 'of some of the grave risks involved in the operation she would never have agreed to it' (<u>Mullins v Parsons</u>,1971,QB). On the other hand in <u>Hatcher v Black</u> the plaintiff, before undergoing the operation of partial thyroidectomy for toxic goitre, asked the surgeon if there was any risk to her voice as she engaged in broadcasting work and required the full use of her voice. He informed her there was none, but her voice was affected by reason of injury to the left recurrent laryngeal nerve. The plaintiff complained that her medical practitioner had been negligent in advising her concerning the operation, and that had she known there was a risk to her voice she would have selected medical treatment and not the operation. Dealing with the failure to inform the patient, it was admitted she had been told there was no risk when it was known that there was a slight risk, but this was done for her good. It was vital that she should not worry. Lord Denning summed up as follows:

He had told a lie which in the circumstances was justifiable. It was a matter in which law was left to the conscience of the doctor himself. The law did not condemn him if he did what a wise doctor so placed would do. (1954,TLR)

In 1975 a court found that although the risk to a patient was real, it was remote and 'as the patient never enquired about the risks the doctor had no obligation to enlighten him' (see,Brazier,1987,p.60). The difficulties faced by patients in these sort of cases was illustrated by the earlier and much quoted case of <u>Bolam v Friern Barnet HMC</u>. Bolam suffered a mental disorder for which he was advised by a consultant psychiatrist to undergo electro-convulsive therapy (ECT). There existed two bodies of medical opinion on the use of relaxant drugs in treatments of this kind. Bolam was admitted to Friern Barnet Hospital and not told of the risks of fracture involved in ECT. During the ECT, Bolam suffered fractures of the acetabulum and pelvis and it was admitted that relaxant drugs would have minimised the risk of fracture. Bolam could not recover for negligence because a doctor cannot be held negligent if he acts in accordance with practice approved by a responsible body of medical men, even though there exist contrasting bodies of medical opinion. Mr.Justice McNair said that a doctor 'is not guilty of negligence if he has acted in accordance with a practice accepted by a responsible body of medical men skilled in that particular art' (<u>Bolam v Friern Barnet HMC</u>,1957,1 W.L.R.,587).
A different view has been formulated in the USA and Canada. In the American case of <u>Canterbury v Spence</u> (464 F.2d 772,780 1972) a different test for 'failure to warn' was accepted. Canterbury had a suspected ruptured disc. The doctor told him that a laminectomy was necessary to correct this and the patient raised no objection and did not enquire about the exact nature of the operation. As a result of the operation, the patient suffered extensive paralysis. The patient sued the doctor for negligence alleging that the doctor had failed to warn him of the risks involved. The court held for the plaintiff concluding that the physician must reveal such information as an average,reasonable patient would deem material to the decision whether or not to consent. The Supreme Court of Canada has followed this principle in <u>Hopp v Lepp</u> (1980,112 DLR (3d) 67) and <u>Riebl v Hughes</u> (1980, 114 DLR (3d) 1). In the former Chief Justice Laskin stated that:

in obtaining the consent of a patient for the performance upon him of a surgical operation, a surgeon, generally, should answer any specific questions posed by the patient as to the risks involved, and should, without being questioned, disclose to him the nature of the proposed operation, its gravity, and material risks and any special or unusual risks attendant upon the performance of the operation. (see,Corner,1985,p.96)

However in the UK, when the House of Lords considered the case of <u>Sidaway v Board of Governors of the Bethlem Royal and the</u>

22

<u>Maudsley Hospital</u> (1985,2 W.L.R.,480), the majority of their Lordships endorsed the view expressed in the Bolam case.

With regard to mistakes in diagnosis and treatment, the former are not necessarily negligent, since mistaken diagnosis is accepted as a risk inherent in the practice of medicine:

> in the realm of diagnosis...there is ample scope for genuine difference of opinion and one clearly is not negligent merely because his conclusion differs from that of other professional men. (Lord Scarman, <u>Maynard v West Midlands RHA</u>,1984, 1 WLR,634)

Mistakes in treatment are more readily accepted by the courts as evidence of negligence. There have, for example, been very few decisions on operating mistakes (eg wrong patient or wrong limb) because they are usually indefensible (see, Martin, 1973, p.366, p.371, p.372). Similarly, if the wrong drug or wrong dosage has been used the patient's claim will usually succeed (see, Brazier,1987,p.79).

(iii) <u>Did the negligence result in damage to the plaintiff?</u>

It is important to remember that it has not only to be proved that the medical practitioner or hospital authority is negligent, but that any injury suffered was a direct consequence of the negligence. This point is illustrated by the case of <u>Barnett v Chelsea and Kensington HMC</u>.

William Barnett was employed by Chelsea College of Science and Technology as a nightwatchman. At 9.30 pm on 31st.December 1965 he reported for duty with two other nightwatchmen. They had a drink to celebrate the New Year. At 4 a.m., one of the men was struck with an iron bar by an intruder and was taken to St.Stephens Hospital. He was seen by a nurse and the casualty officer; his head was dressed and he was told to report for X-ray at 9.45 a.m.. Barnett then drove his mate back to College. At 5 a.m., the three watchmen shared some tea; immediately after Barnett complained of the heat in the room; 20 minutes later all were vomiting. At 8 a.m. when the day workers arrived at college they drove back to St.Stephens in Barnett's car. They went to the casualty department and complained that they had all vomited continuously since drinking the tea. One of the men - not Barnett who was saying nothing at this time - demanded that they see a doctor. The nurse's impression was that they had all been drinking alcohol to excess. However she telephoned the doctor and the following conversation ensued:

Nurse: Is that the medical casualty officer? There are three men complaining of vomiting after drinking tea.
Doctor: Well I am vomiting myself and I have not been drinking. Tell them to go home and go to bed and call their own doctors.

The nurse relayed this message to the men who then left and went back to the college. Later in the morning Barnett was seen by a member of the college staff looking ill. A doctor was called and Barnett was taken to hospital but was dead on arrival at 2 pm on 1st.January,1966.

Mrs.Barnett sued the hospital claiming that death resulted from the defendant's negligence in not diagnosing or treating his condition when he presented himself at the casualty department.The judgment in the case was as follows.

Firstly, the court held that:

> since the defendants provided and ran the casualty department to which the deceased presented himself complaining of illness or injury, such a close and direct relationship existed between him and them that they owed him a duty to exercise the skill and care to be expected of a nurse and medical casualty officer acting reasonably, notwithstanding that he had not been treated and received into the hospital wards.

So the court was quite clear that the defendants owed a legal duty to the plaintiff to exercise care in their conduct.

Secondly, the court held that:

> the medical casualty officer was negligent in not seeing and not examining the deceased, in not admitting him to the wards, and in not treating him or causing him to be treated, and that accordingly the defendants were in breach of their duty to the deceased.

The court was also quite clear that the defendants had acted in a negligent manner.

However having regard to the medical evidence about the impossibility of a quick diagnosis of arsenical poisoning the judgment concluded that:

> since..(Mr.Barnett)...must have died of the poisoning even if he had been admitted to the wards five hours before his death and treated with all care, the plaintiff had failed to establish on the balance of probabilities that the defendant's negligence had caused the death, and that, therefore, the claim failed'. (<u>Barnett v Chelsea and Kensington HMC</u>, 1968, 1 All E.R.,pp.1068-74)

In this case the loss or damage was undisputed; and the court found that there had been a clear case of negligence. But whilst both negligence and loss constitute part of a short sequence of related events, it was concluded that the negligence was not the cause of the loss. For an action to be successful for the plaintiff, the court not only has to be satisfied that the balance of probabilities indicates a duty of care, a case of negligence, and a loss or damage suffered, but that all three can be linked together in a direct causal relationship.

Conclusions

> The first thing we do, let's kill all the lawyers.
> William Shakespeare, <u>Second Part of Henry VI</u>, Act 4,
> Scene 2

> Sure there's such a thing as law. We're up to our necks in
> it, about all it does is make business for lawyers.
> Raymond Chandler, <u>The Long Goodbye</u>, Penguin Books,
> Harmondsworth, 1959, p.267.

Complaints about the law courts have a long history. 'There has
never been a time when law courts have been free from
complaints; complaints have been about delay, costs, vexations,
elements in procedure, incompetent administration and generally
inconvenient and inefficient arrangements of courts (Jackson,
1977, pp.64-65, see also Civil Justice Review, 1988, p.12).
Given the number and range of cases dealt with by the courts it
is not easy to present a full and fair review of the workings
of this system of dealing with medical negligence. However
attention can be directed at a number of questions about the
efficacy and equity of the system. In particular a number of
arguments can be developed against the value of court
proceedings in such cases.

Firstly, there is the fairness of judicial proceedings and
their reliance on crucial decisions made by judges regarding
what does, and what does not, constitute negligence. There was
a time when juries assessed damages for personal injuries - a
situation which still prevails in the USA. The modern practice
of 'reasoned awards by judges' has been described as a
'substantial advance on the inscrutable awards of juries' (Lord
Scarman, <u>Lim Poh Choo v Camden Health Authority</u>, 1979 2 All
ER,p.917). Whether the decisions of judges are 'more reasoned'
and 'less inscrutable' than juries may well be disputed.
Referring to the final example used in their analysis of
judgements in the House of Lords, Murphy and Rawlings commented
on the 'highly elusive' and 'strangely evanescent quality' of
a speech by Lord Diplock, concluding that there was 'a
disturbing side to the spectacle....the absence of any serious
discussion of the arguments of one side'. Overall their
analysis highlights the role of a range of 'discursive
techniques' in the development of the arguments they reviewed,
including 'repetition, assertion, the use of common sense, the
invocation of the ordinary man, silence and suppression'
(Murphy and Rawlings,1982,p.57).

There is also the long-standing argument that the neutrality
of the judiciary is a myth (see, for example, Griffith, 1977,
pp.189-92, and Miliband, 1973, pp.124-30); and it has been
suggested that 'for a long time the judges were most unwilling
to find against a medical man..a brotherly solidarity bound the
ancient professions of law and medicine (Brazier, 1987, p.69).
Whether it is judges or juries who are best placed to determine
the outcome of medical negligence cases, for the moment in the
UK it is the former who are going to be responsible for
establishing a number of important principles in the light of
which many cases will be decided.

Secondly, it can be argued that 'legal tests' and 'legal concepts' limit the effectiveness of court proceedings. The case of <u>Barnett v Chelsea and Kensington HMC</u> illustrated that a duty of care, negligence and a loss or injury all have to be established and linked. In that case court proceedings were ineffective in responding to what the court itself found to be a clear case of negligence. In the case of <u>Whitehouse v Jordan</u> court proceedings could in the end offer nothing in recompense for the profound losses suffered, because the causal actions were found not to constitute negligence. This is not to suggest that the conclusions of the courts were wrong in these cases, but to illustrate that if as a society we wish to take some action in cases of medical negligence (<u>Barnett v Chelsea and Kensington HMC</u>) or medical accidents (<u>Whitehouse v Jordan</u>), court proceedings constitute a limited and possibly ineffective response in some cases. Some of the major objections to using court proceedings is that judicial decisions are based on such factors as the degree of blame attaching to a defendant's conduct and the degree of contributory negligence by the plaintiff. Both of these considerations may have a very limited relationship to the needs of the plaintiff.

Thirdly, there is the problem of access to judicial welfare. We do not know how knowledgeable the general public are about the possibility of taking cases of medical negligence through the courts. The publicity given in the Press to the more spectacular settlements may mean that most people have some awareness of this avenue of redress. It has been suggested that recent figures represent an increasing 'claims consciousness' - that contemporary attitudes are best exemplified by the man under the Clapham omnibus who wishes to lay the blame on someone else for his current predicament! (see, for example, Dingwall,Fenn and Harris, 1988, p.15). Whether individuals are actually able to use the system if they do know about it, may be significantly influenced by the effectiveness and fairness of statutory provision for legal aid and advice. Without such provision many individuals may be deterred by the cost of litigation which is often quite disproportionate to the amount involved in a claim. The legal costs of both parties to a personal injury case which goes to trial can often equal or exceed the damages recovered (see, Civil Justice Review, 1988, para.69); they were estimated at £1 million in a recent case (Pannick,1988). Fear of costs certainly appears to be one of the greatest deterrents to using the courts (Civil Justice Review,1988,para 70). It seems probable that the current low level of means tests creates an effective 'income-bar' for many individuals and that the 'reasonableness test' may have a rather arbitrary effect on the cases that are accepted for legal aid (see, Society of Labour Lawyers, 1978, pp.7-8). The latter may be particularly noticeable given the admitted difficulties in deciding some cases of medical negligence. If the necessary financial resources are available to potential plaintiffs, they will also require specialist legal advice and this is not always readily available. This was illustrated by the case of the man irreversibly brain-damaged by negligent hospital treatment in 1976 who was awarded £491,682 in the High Court, five years after his former solicitors had advised his parents to settle for £2000 (The Guardian,2 August,1988). We should also note that there may be considerable inequalities in the ability of different groups of the population to use the courts - issues of knowledge and costs, both in money and time, being especially relevant.

Fourthly, there are the court proceedings themselves. Issues here include the adversarial nature, the delays, the uncertainties and once again the costs of these proceedings. It can be argued that the legal proceedings as currently constituted in the UK tend, through their adversarial approach, to generate hostility between parties and so reduce the likelihood of reaching either a speedy or mutually satisfactory resolution of disputes. It has been pointed out that 'the atmosphere engendered by litigation, with an individual doctor with his back to the wall so to speak, is not the best means of investigating..a complex issue' (Brazier,1987,p.64). Hostility may be regarded as inevitable in alleged cases of medical negligence. But there is evidence that many complainants about medical treatment are not seeking financial redress but rather to prevent the reoccurrence of distressing events (see,for example,Select Committee on the Parliamentary Commissioner for Administration,1985,p.4). In such cases the aims of the complainants are not going to be well served by becoming plaintiffs in an adversarial system.

The problem of delay was illustrated by the Whitehouse v Jordan case which took over eleven years to resolve and the decision of the House of Lords in March 1988, to order a retrial of a personal injury claim arising out of a premature birth of a baby in 1978 (Wilsher v Essex AHA, 1988, W.L.R.,25 March). The study undertaken for the Review Body on Civil Justice found that in personal injury cases, High Court cases frequently take four, five, six or more years from incident to conclusion, a situation which was not helped by it taking the best part of a year in the High Court after the two sides were ready for trial, before a judge could be made available; but in addition cases which were settled by agreement took as long as those which went to trial (see, Civil Justice Review, 1988, para.432).

It may justifiably be said that

> the ancient rules of the English Common Law have as one of their notable virtues the characteristic that in general they can never be said to be finally limited by definition but have rather the capacity of adaptation in accordance with the changing circumstances of succeeding ages. (Lord Evershed, Haley v London Electricity Board,1965,A.C.778)

This flexibility of the Common Law is however also allied to a certain degree of inconsistency, for example there are occasions when the court says that

> the social or economic consequences of...(a)...particular solution to a dispute or the establishment of some principle which might affect other cases are not its concern...at other times, the court is quite prepared to discuss what social or economic policy ought to be; it is

a charming but infuriating characteristic of the common law that it offers no guidance as to which of these devices it will use in any particular case. (Jacob and Davies,1987,p.1-38)

When these characteristics of the Common Law are allied to the characteristics of judgments in the House of Lords (see,Murphy and Rawlings,1981,1982) the plaintiff is presented with a degree of uncertainty inherent in the system that is not altogether reassuring to one who is considering embarking on the nerve-wracking and time-consuming business of a court case. These uncertainties may be seen to be perhaps greater in cases of medical negligence than other negligence or personal injury cases; such cases present quite specific problems associated with the delay in obtaining a clear prognosis where injury has been suffered as a result of treatment, and the possible difficulty of obtaining expert evidence against a medical practitioner (see,for example, O'Connell,1975,p.30). Although with regard to the latter Lord Denning commented on the Whitehouse v Jordan case as follows:

It is sometimes said that you cannot get one medical man to give evidence against another, just as it is said that you cannot get one lawyer to give evidence against another. This case shows how wrong that is. In this case two of the most eminent obstetricians in the country have given evidence against the surgeon; and two equally eminent men have given evidence for him. (see,1980,1 All E,R.,p.653)

The problem of uncertainty is illustrated by the Sidaway case which leaves the law unclear on the issue of disclosure given the emphasis placed by some of the law lords on the patient's failure to seek information about the risks. What test governs the doctor's duty of disclosure to the more curious and enquiring patients? (see,Brazier,1987,pp.65-66).

The issue of costs arises again, and as more than an issue for the complainant. Doctors have expressed concern about the decision of the Medical Protection Society to introduce risk-related subscriptions for 1989 with those working in some specialities facing almost four-fold increases in premiums (Ham,1988). These increased subscriptions reflect the rising bill for compensation in medical negligence claims in the UK. According to the Medical Defence Union claims against doctors have risen by 60% in three years alongside the rising level of awards (see Table 2.1, p.29), and it is the community at large who contribute a significant proportion of the costs involved in cases of alleged medical negligence dealt with by the courts.

This contribution is partly a clear and explicit contribution from public expenditure on such items as court administration and legal services. Furthermore, in so far as costs are also met from various forms of insurance, then these insurance premiums may also be met directly or indirectly from public expenditure. The Government reimburses GPs subscriptions to the defence societies and subscriptions paid by NHS hospital doctors are tax-allowable. In addition, claims are directed

28

against health authorities as well as doctors, with research indicating significant increases in claims over the past decade (see, The Guardian, 25.3.88; see also, Dingwall, Fenn and Harris, 1988, p.9). Significant public contributions to a system where the 'lion's share of the total costs..(of the system)..goes to the legal community' (O'Connell,1975,p.42) and which may not produce definitive decisions on key cases for several years, may also constitute a basis for public reservations about the courts as institutions for reviewing cases of medical negligence.

Table 2.1
Highest awards in medical negligence claims in the UK

1979 : £220,000
     : £229,298 (Lim Poh Choo v Camden & Islington AHA)
     : £262,000
1981 : £311,562
1982 : £398,629
1985 : £413,943
     : £580,547
1986 : £679,264
1987 : £1,032,000 (Aboul-Hosn)

Source: N.Timmins,1987, C.Hicks.1987

Fifthly, there are the outcomes of the judicial process for the individuals concerned and the wider community. The hope for the complainant must be compensation if a loss has been suffered as a result of negligent acts. But only three out of those ten who seek compensation receive a payment (Ham,1988). What of the payments that are made - do they constitute fair compensation for complainants? This would be difficult to discern, even if one had ready access to all the relevant cases. There is no doubt that the assessment of monetary compensation for non-monetary loss is inherently difficult. The court's task is aided by the existence of a tariff which relates to particular classes of injury and is derived from reported court decisions. But 'the application of the tariff itself may be complex and highly variable from case to case' (Civil Justice Review,1988,para.399). More generally there are issues of what allowance should be made for such items as loss of future earnings, the cost of future care, and for future inflation; all remain contentious items. . Once again there is the problem of the delay in receipt of damages that may be awarded. In Lim Poh Choo v Camden and Islington AHA, Lord Scarman commented as follows:

> The course of the litigation illustrates with devastating clarity, the insuperable problems implicit in a system of compensation for personal injuries which (unless the parties agree otherwise) can yield only a lump sum assessed by the court at the time of judgement...the award is final; it is not susceptible to review as the future unfolds, substituting fact for estimate. Knowledge of the future being denied to mankind, so much of the award is to be

attributed to future loss and suffering...(and)...will almost certainly be wrong. There is really only one certainty: the future will prove the award to be either too high or too low. (1979,2 All ER,p.914)

The summary of the House of Lords judgement in this case concluded that 'a radical reappraisal and reform of the law relating to personal injury is required' (1979,2 All ER,p.912).
For the wider community there are concerns about the impact on medical practice. The hope must be that the pursuit of cases of medical negligence through the courts will establish and maintain good, sound standards of medical practice. However it is far from clear that court actions have any tangible, desirable effect in terms of preventing negligent acts and promoting good practice. The case of <u>Bolam v Friern Barnet HMC</u> reminds us that widely adopted practices, precisely because they are widespread in the profession, cannot be regarded as negligent even if harm results to a patient. <u>Maynard v West Midlands RHA</u> provided a more recent example of this principle when Lord Scarman stated that:

It is not enough to show that subsequent events show that the operation need never have been performed, if at the time the decision to operate was taken it was reasonable in the sense that a responsible body of medical opinion would have accepted it as proper. (<u>Maynard v West Midlands RHA</u>, 1985, 1 All E.R. 635)

This does not mean that a profession can simply set its own standard of reasonable care. Court proceedings for medical negligence may speed the process by which 'unsatisfactory practices' are eliminated (see, Martin, 1973,pp.358-359); and when the Sidaway case was heard in the Court of Appeal, Donaldson stated that:

the definition of the duty of care was a matter for the law and the courts could not stand idly by if the profession, by an excess of paternalism, denied their patients real choice. The law would not permit the medical profession to play God. (Law Report, The Times, 24 February,1984,p.24)

It is clear that the legal concept of negligence is not an especially dynamic force for improving practice. Indeed it has been suggested that not only does tort 'not encourage prevention', but that fears of malpractice suits may lead to unsafe practices (see, O'Connell, 1975,,pp.22-24 and pp.42-43).It is argued that a tendency to make doctors liable for every diagnostic error may cause patients to be submitted to more expensive and potentially risky procedures than may be strictly medically desirable (Brazier,1987,p.78). Furthermore, experienced practitioners in the USA 'are known to have refused to treat patients for fear of being accused of negligence' (Lord Denning, <u>Whitehouse v Jordan</u>,1980,1 All E.R.p.658). The end result may be legally defensive medicine, defined by the US Dept of Health,Education and Welfare as:

the conducting of a test or performance of a diagnostic or therapeutic procedure which is not medically justified but is carried out primarily (if not solely) to prevent or defend against the threat of medico-legal liability. (US Dept.of Health, Education and Welfare, 1973)

Legally defensive medicine may lead to fundamental changes in medical practice; as actions in the USA against obstetricians have become more common so the rate of Caesarian sections has increased (Brazier,1987,p.70). For the UK it has been argued that 'defensive medicine is practised in fear of a perceived and frequently unreal foe' involving 'medical misconceptions of legal responsibility' (Finch,1986,p.15). However if 'defensivism' is pursued there is little doubt that it can make yet another contribution to the costs of 'the system'. It has been estimated that one in every three X-rays in the USA may be undertaken for legal reasons (O'Connell,1975,p.43).

In conclusion a fundamental concern with court proceedings remains that it may be impossible to prove negligence where it is clear that medical intervention has left the plaintiffs and/or their dependants in a disadvantaged state. That this situation is unsatisfactory was the view of Lawton LJ in Whitehouse v Jordan when he concluded that:

As long as liability in this type of case rests on proof of fault, judges will have to go on making decisions which they would prefer not to make. The victims of medical mishaps of this kind should, in my opinion, be cared for by the community, not by the hazards of litigation. (1980,1 All E.R.,pp.661-662)

In a similar vein an American writer concluded that

it is time we turned to ambitious legislation for reform instead of relying so much on the tortured, tortuous, even torturing tort system with its case by case common-law crawl - a system from which law professors derive so much fascination, law practitioners so much income, and the general public so few benefits. (O'Connell,1975,p.67)

Given these criticisms of the courts (judicial welfare) as a means of compensating for medical negligence, we might justifiably ask whether alternative administrative arrangements between government, the profession and the health service might offer more attractive alternatives to the complainant ? The next two chapters will consider some of these alternatives which have been established in the UK.

3 Outside the courts: state intervention in medicine and health care

Over a period of slightly less than ninety years three Acts of Parliament extended state intervention into the affairs of medical practitioners and the provision of health services. The first, the Medical Act,1858, established what we now know as the General Medical Council with powers to regulate the medical profession. The second, the National Insurance Act,1911 established a system by which the services of general medical practitioners were made available to a significant number of British working-class men. The third, the National Health Service Act, 1946, provided the statutory basis for the establishment of the National Health Service in 1948. Each extension of state activity opened up a new avenue for redress for at least some patients grievances, and so complemented the older remedy of 'going to law' with an action for negligence.

In this chapter we examine each of these new avenues in turn. We shall seek to explain something of the manner in which they have operated and to indicate some of the reservations which have been expressed about their mode of operation.

General Medical Council

The functions of the General Medical Council (GMC) include maintaining a register of all those entitled to practice and ensuring appropriate educational standards for those qualifying for the profession. The disciplinary powers of the GMC - which include the power to suspend or erase the name of a medical practitioner from the Medical Register - were established by

Section 28, Medical Act,1858.
   The disciplinary powers of the GMC have been continued and amended in subsequent legislation (The Medical Acts of 1950, 1956, 1969 and 1978), the most recent changes being incorporated in Sections 36, 38, 40, 42, and 43 of the Medical Act, 1983. The Medical Act, 1978, was primarily concerned with the implementation of a number of proposals contained in the Report of the Committee of Enquiry into the Regulation of the Medical Profession (Merrison Report,1975). These included changes in the composition of the GMC. (see Table 3.1)

Table 3.1
Composition of the GMC before and after the Medical Act, 1978

Total membership		Elected (i)	Appointed (ii)	Nominated (iii)	Professional members
(A)	47	11	28	8	(44)
(B)	98	54	34	10	(88)
(C)	94/95	50	34	10/11	(89)
(D)	97	50	34	13	(86)

(i)   elected by registered medical practitioners
(ii) appointed by the universities and the licensing bodies
(iii) nominated by the Crown (The Privy Council)

(A) - situation prior to Medical Act,1978; five of the nominated members were members of the medical profession. (B) - recommendation of the Merrison Report,1975,para.390; none
   of the nominated members were to be members of the medical profession.
(C) - situation after the Medical Act,1978; Section 1 of the
   Act specifies that the elected members shall be in the
   majority over the appointed and nominated members. The actual numbers were set out in an order of the Privy Council dated 3/2/79 which specified that the majority of
   the nominated members shall be lay members (see SI 1979/112).
(D) - GMC membership,1988
NB All elected and appointed members are members of the medical profession.

   Until 1950 the disciplinary function was exercised by the GMC itself. It subsequently became the sole responsibility of the GMC Disciplinary Committee and then, following the Medical Act,1978, the Professional Conduct Committee; these committees being constituted by statute and formed from the body of the GMC, with procedures governed by the GMC Disciplinary Committee (Procedure) Rules,1970. The Professional Conduct Committee must include one lay member. Apart from the change of name, the Preliminary Proceedings Committee acquired the additional power of interim suspension. This was recommended by the Merrison Committee for cases where

      there was clear evidence to suggest that ... (a
      practitioner's) ... continued registration, for however
      short a time, would be a serious danger to the public.
      (Merrison Report,1975,para.292)

33

The GMC disciplinary system runs parallel to the courts, that is to say a court action does not preclude taking a case to the GMC or vice versa, although they are concerned with different issues - should there be compensation (the courts) and should the doctor be in practice (the GMC). However, if an action is pending in the High Court an application can be made to the Court for an order of prohibition to forbid the Professional Conduct Committee to proceed until the court action has been dispensed with (see, for example, Tarnesby v GMC, 1969, 1 Q.B.,C.C.,A.C.A.,The Times).

By the same token disciplinary action by the health authorities does not preclude GMC action and indeed one means by which cases of serious professional misconduct, including possible cases of medical negligence, come to the notice of the GMC is through a practitioner being subjected to a deduction from his remuneration as a family practitioner in the National Health Service. There is a DHSS/RHA agreement about the notification of the GMC with regard to statutory proceedings concerning general practitioners (see,Merrison Report,1975,para.229). There is also DHSS guidance to hospitals on this matter, but the Merrison Committee noted that 'in practice NHS hospital authorities do not notify convictions and very rarely report other matters to the GMC' (Merrison Report,1975,para.230). This situation appears to have persisted with the effect that the GMC is much more effectively informed about cases concerning GPs than those concerning hospital doctors (Robinson,1988,pp.15-16). This has led the President of the GMC to state that the GMC is 'less satisfied with the mechanisms by which outcomes of complaints procedures in the hospital services are reported to us' (quoted by Robinson, 1988, p.23).

Proceedings are not initiated by the Council itself, unlike the Pharmaceutical Society which has its own inspectorate (see,Klein and Shinebourne,1972,p.400), but from matters brought to its notice, including the receipt of a complaint by a member of the public. The procedures for dealing with complaints are shown in Figure 3.1.(see, p.35). In the period September 1983 to August 1987 the GMC received 3821 complaints. Figure 3.1 also indicates the small proportion of these complaints that reach the final stages of the GMC procedures.

Particular concern has been expressed about those complaints that do not reach the Preliminary Screener on the grounds that they involve complaints about medical care in the NHS. Although there is nothing in the Medical Act which says the GMC may or should require complainants to use the NHS complaints systems first, it appears that the 'policy of the GMC for the past 15 years has been in effect to use the NHS as the primary sifting mechanism' (Robinson,1988,p.8). A recent analysis undertaken by the GMC's staff indicated that in one five month period 43% of complaints about hospital doctors and GPS were effectively referred back to the NHS (Robinson,1988,p.21). Whilst there appears to be a certain logic to adopting a mechanism to avoid cases being examined in parallel by separate institutions, this GMC policy has not been widely publicised and does seem to ignore the widespread criticisms that have been addressed to the complaints systems in the NHS (see, pp.39-52).

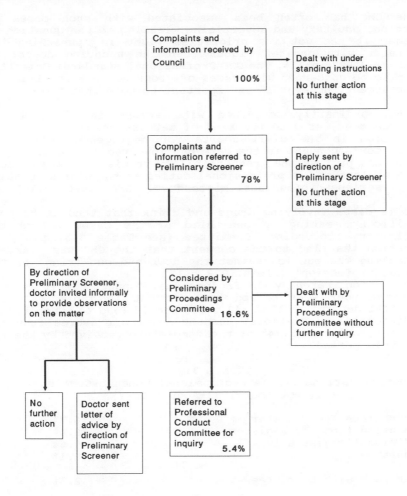

The figures in boxes represent the proportion of cases reaching various stages in the system, beginning with all the complaints and information received (represented by 100%) and the percentage of these cases that are passed on to : (1) Preliminary screener (78%) who is either the President of the GMC or a member of the GMC nominated by the President; (2) Preliminary Proceedings Committee (16.6%); (3) Professional Conduct Committee (5.4%). The latter (2 & 3) include lay members of the GMC.

Figures are based on complaints received by the GMC between September 1983 and August 1987.

Figure 3.1 Procedures for dealing with complaints received by
          the GMC
Source : General Medical Council, Annual Reports (1984, 1985,
          1986, 1987)

The GMC has often been associated with such cases as abortion, adultery and advertising, leading to the question of whether it has got its priorities right in 'punishing the adulterer with greater vigour than the uncaring doctor ?' (Brazier, 1987, p.11). The GMC Professional Standards Committee can also be concerned with cases of gross neglect in diagnosis or treatment. However it is important to note that the GMC is:

> not ordinarily concerned with errors in diagnosis or treatment, or with the kind of matters which give rise to action in the civil courts for negligence unless the doctor's conduct in the case has involved such a disregard of his professional responsibility to his patients or such a neglect of his professional duties as to raise a question of serious professional misconduct. (GMC, 1985, p.10)

It is cases involving drugs and drink that tend to be more significant, making up one-third of the cases before the Preliminary Proceedings Committee (see Table 3.3, p.36), a situation that led to the comment that the GMC was 'largely protecting the public against the down and out fringe of the medical profession' (Klein,1973,p.173).

The actions taken by the Professional Conduct Committee over a recent four year period are set out in Table 3.2. The Committee determined that 143 cases should lead to admonitions, conditional registrations, suspensions and erasures from the Register; this was 3.74% of the complaints received by the GMC over this period.

Table 3.2
Determinations of the Professional Conduct Committee
(September 1983-August 1987)

Erasure from the Register	16.7%
Suspension from the Register	19.0%
Conditional registration	9.6%
Admonishment	25.1%
Refer to health Committee	2.3%
Postponed/adjourned	7.4%
Not guilty	23.7%
TOTAL NUMBER OF CASES	210

Sources: GMC Annual Reports,1984,1985,1986,1987.

The Medical Act, 1950 introduced for the first time the statutory right of appeal to the Judicial Committee of the Privy Council. Before 1950, appeals against erasure from the register could only be made on questions of law or complete disregard of the principle of 'natural justice' and appeal was to the High Court. In practice the Privy Council takes the view that it would require a very strong case to interfere with the sentence on a charge of professional misconduct on the

Table 3.3
Analysis of cases dealt with by the GMC
(Sep.1983 - Aug.1987)

	Preliminary Proceedings Committee	Professional Standards Committee
Disregard of prof. responsibilities to patients	24.4%	40.9%
Abuse of alcohol	20.7%	0.95%
Dishonesty	10.9%	14.8%
Other cases	9.9%	4.8%
Advertising,canvassing or depreciation	7.4%	5.7%
Abuse of drugs	6.9%	1.9%
Improper prescribing for others of drugs of addiction	4.5%	12.8%
Violence	3.3%	1.42%
Indecency	3.1%	4.8%
Personal relationships of an emotional or sexual nature with a patient	3.1%	5.2%
False certification or signing unverified statements	2.8%	0.95%
Breach of professional confidence	1.3%	0.95%
False claim to qualifications or status	1.0%	1.42%
Improper delegation of professional duties	0.6%	2.84%
Use of abusive or rude language to patients or professional colleagues	0.1%	0.0%
Obstructing course of justice	0.0%	1.42%
TOTAL NOS.OF CASES	706	210

Sources: GMC Annual Reports,1984,1985,1986,1987

understanding that a committee of the GMC are the best possible people for weighing the seriousness of the professional misconduct (see, for example, Chandra Bhattacharya v GMC, 1969, The Times; and McCoan v GMC, 1964, 1 W.L.R., 1147).

The doctor's right of appeal to the Judicial Committee of the Privy Council remained in the new legislation (see, Section 11 of the Medical Act, 1978), but the legislation confers no right of appeal on those who have complained about a particular doctor's conduct. The Merrison Committee commented on this as follows:

> Our view is that the nature of fitness to practice proceedings rules out a right of appeal for complainants. The aim of the GMC's fitness to practice controls is to protect the general public, not provide for some sort of adversarial consideration of the merits of two opposing

points of view; and the civil courts, not the GMC, are the places for an individual to seek personal redress against a doctor. If the GMC is satisfied at any stage that the matter brought before it does not raise a question of fitness to practice there seems no good reason for the exercise of its discretion in any particular case to be brought into question by an individual member of the public who, unlike the doctor, is not at immediate risk of losing his livelihood. (Merrison Report, 1975, para.319)

The doctor's right to apply for restoration to the Medical register after erasure was also continued in the legislation (see,Medical Act,1978,Section 14). As before such applications can be made after 10 months have elapsed. Finally, whilst legal aid is still denied to complainants, the 1978 legislation confirmed the right of legal representation to both complainant and practitioner.

Conclusions

It is the general public who are the major source of complaints reaching the GMC. As with the more spectacular court cases, media coverage may create and sustain public knowledge of the GMC as an avenue of complaint; although the evidence received by the Merrison Committee showed considerable misunderstanding of the GMC's disciplinary procedures (see,Merrison Report, 1975, Appendix C, p165). Lodging a complaint with the GMC is not a course of action to be lightly undertaken. Whilst the 1978 legislation confirmed the right of legal representation to both complainant and practitioner, the absence of legal aid to the potential complainant may obviously be a significant deterrent to many individuals. Furthermore, as the Merrison Committee noted

    since the standard of evidence required to prove a charge before the Disciplinary Committee equates with the standard required in a criminal court, the institution of proceedings involves very considerable work and expense. (Merrison Report,1975,para.255)

As it is, the vast majority of cases do not reach the Professional Conduct Committee - a situation that has remained constant over the years (see Klein, 1973, pp.173-4; Bewley, 1988; Robinson, 1988, p.6; see also, Figure 3.1 above); this has led to the criticism that the GMC 'has been able to hold itself aloof from most complaints about the quality of medical care' (Robinson, 1988, p.13). It has been suggested that this 'elaborate sifting process' may include some concern about the 'winnability' of cases given the cost of full hearings in lawyers' fees and members' time (Klein,1973,pp.173-74).

Of particular significance is the apparent reliance of the GMC on the NHS complaints systems. Apart from concerns about the efficacy of these systems, there is the additional point that this procedure may lead to a situation where the original complainant is not then necessarily 'the complainant for GMC purposes' (the health authority concerned becomes the complainant). This results in loss of certain rights that are afforded to the complainant (see, Robinson, 1988, p.27).

Other comments about the operation of the GMC are that it acts as both prosecutor, judge, jury and executioner (see, Klein and Shinebourne, 1972, p.401 and Savage, 1987), and that the decision of a largely professional body relating to a member of that profession is likely to be tinged with bias (Martin, 1973,p.46). The 'sifting process' can certainly be criticised not only because the majority of complaints are rejected by one person (Preliminary Screener) but also that there is no lay involvement in this process (Robinson, 1988, p.14)

Finally, there is the point of what the GMC actually does. Reference has already been made to the standard of proof required - 'beyond reasonable doubt' not the 'balance of probabilities' that is required in negligence cases heard by the courts (see,Chapter Two). To this can be added the dilemma that 'it is not negligence, nor an isolated failure in caring that constitutes serious misconduct' (Brazier,1987,p.12) and the further concern that the standard for 'serious professional misconduct' (which Robinson contrasts with the 'professional misconduct' which applies to the nursing profession, see, Robinson, 1988, pp.39-40) is so high that the GMC are unlikely to find many doctors guilty of such conduct (Brazier, 1987, p.12-13).

The suspension or erasure of the medical practitioner's name from the Medical Register obviously involves considerable loss to the practitioner. But as we have already indicated it is an outcome for only a small number of cases (recently between 18 and 21 cases a year, see GMC, Annual Reports, 1984, 1985, 1986, 1987). Furthermore, it does not recompense the patient for any inconvenience or loss that he or she may have suffered. The practitioner's ability both to appeal and to apply for restoration to the Register if struck off, may make the daunting task of preparing a case for the GMC seem to be hardly worth the effort.

National Health Service complaints machinery

Family practitioner services

It is difficult to imagine a system more confusing, tortuous, slow and expensive.
K.Bell,1969,p.1975

The system of administering general practitioner services established by the National Insurance Act,1911 must rank as one of the more durable political compromises in the history of British social policy. And the same can be said of the complaints machinery which was established as part of the system in 1912 and which 'in broad outline...(was)...the system which was still in operation 60 years later' (Klein,1973). The establishment of this complaints machinery meant that from 1912 onwards there were from the patient's point of view, three avenues of pursuing cases of medical negligence - at least for the 'panel patients', the increasing proportion of the population who were covered by the National Health Insurance scheme.

These procedures have been able to deal with almost all serious complaints, including allegations that a practitioner has failed to exercise a proper degree of skill, knowledge and care in the exercise of professional judgement (see, Secretary of State for Social Services, 1987, para.8.2), and their use has never precluded a complainant from taking a case to the GMC or through the courts.

The history of the National Health Insurance (up to July,1948) / National Health Service (from July 1948) general practitioner complaints system was described as a 'history of non-evolution' (Klein,1973). By the time the Franks Committee on Administrative Tribunals was collecting evidence, both the BMA and the Ministry of Health appeared to have united in support of the scheme; and it was noted that 'of all the sections of the Franks Report, that dealing with the NHS had least effect' (Klein,1973,p.97). The result was to leave in place a system that was attracting a growing body of criticism (see comment by Bell,1969,above; see also, Robson, 1956, Allen, 1956, p.8, Street, 1968, p.57). The Council on Tribunals also took an interest in the workings of the system (see,for example, Council on Tribunals (1965), para.470); but they seemed to be 'more effective in drawing attention to defects in the system than in getting them remedied' (Klein,1973,p.100).

Some writers suggested that some aspects were better under the 1911-1948 National Health Insurance scheme (see, for example, Bell, 1969, p.62 and Klein, 1973, p.69). Certainly consumer representation might be regarded as more effective. The Act of 1936 fixed the membership of each Insurance Committee (the NHI equivalent of the FPC) at a minimum of twenty and maximum of forty, of whom three-fifths were insured persons, one-fifth members of county and county borough councils, and one-fifth medical representatives (Martin, 1979, p.52).

What was in place under the National Health Service has been described as a set of 'labyrinthine arrangements' (Wraith and Hutchesson,1973,p.48). It seems certain to be bewildering to the complainant - the process can have up to fourteen stages in some cases as set out below. The complainant's understanding of proceedings is unlikely to be helped by the fact that individual complaints are investigated in reference to breaches of contract (the contract the GP has with the FPC). A patient's complaint might involve the following stages

(1)   Complaint by patient

(2)   Informal mediation

(3)   Review by Chairman of Family Practitioner Committee (FPC)

(4)   Hearing by the FPC Medical Services Committee

(5)   Report of the Medical Services Committee to FPC

(6) FPC Action, including recommendations to the Secretary of State; this might involve (7)

(7) Reference to NHS Tribunal

(8) NHS Tribunal makes decision

(9) Appeal to Secretary of State

(10) Secretary of State appoints person to hear appeal

(11) Appeal is heard

(12) Report to Secretary of State

(13) Referral to Medical Advisory Committee

(14) Decision by the Secretary of State

The informal procedure for considering complaints by patients was introduced in April 1968, following negotiations between the Minister of Health and the medical profession. The profession had argued that the service committee procedure was unduly cumbersome for dealing with unimportant complaints. Each Executive Council was asked to appoint one of its lay members to operate this procedure of informal mediation - but not all chose to do so.

A service committee need not have a hearing of a complaint if it considers that the complaint is frivolous or vexatious, although the Chairman must bring a case before the Committee and obtain its consent before a hearing can be dispensed with. The practitioner, complainant and any witnesses are invited to committee hearings (Stage 4) which are in private with no representation by counsel, solicitor or paid advocate. However it should be noted that a representative of the medical defence societies can attend as 'a friend' of the doctor. A service committee reports to the FPC (Stage 5), stating such relevant facts as appear to have been established, the inferences which may be drawn from them, and recommending what action, if any, should be taken. The latter normally consists of one of the following:

no further action (generally where the breach of contract is trivial);

a warning;

the recovery from the practitioner, and repayment to the person concerned, of expenses reasonably and necessarily incurred by the person owing to the failure of the practitioner to comply with the FPC terms of service; or

the withholding of an amount from the respondent's remuneration.

41

Following the FPC's decision, the practitioner or complainant has the right to appeal to the Secretary of State who may determine the appeal either on the papers or after an oral hearing, with the practitioner being automatically entitled to the latter if the FPC proposes withholding remuneration. The hearing is private and is conducted by a legally qualified chairman from the Department of Health and two members of the same profession as the practitioner. Parties to the appeal are entitled to be legally represented at appeal hearings.

The NHS Tribunal considers representations that the continued inclusion of a person on any FPC list would be prejudicial to the efficiency of the service (Stage 7, see pp.40/1). The Tribunal's Chairman must be a practising barrister or solicitor of not less than ten years' standing. There are two other members, both appointed by the Secretary of State, one from a panel of medical practitioners. Procedure is at the Tribunal's discretion, but is normally in private. An appeal (by the practitioner) against the Tribunal's decision is decided by the Secretary of State in the light of the report of a hearing by persons he appoints for the purpose (Stage 13, see pp.40/1).

In the absence of legal aid, and the regulation which specifically excludes the participation of counsel, solicitor or paid advocate in the first six stages, the burden is 'almost entirely on the complainant to collect his evidence, marshall his witnesses and present his case' (Klein,1973,p.137). The resulting situation was described as follows:

> throughout the proceedings, practitioners receive the backing of their professional defence unions and are advised and represented by counsel, whereas ordinary citizens depending on their own resources can rarely afford either legal advice or representation. (Bell,1969,p.71)

Other interesting features of the procedures are that in cases which go to the NHS Tribunal only the medical practitioner has the right of appeal (Stage 9, see pp.40/1) perhaps on the same rationale that governs the GMC procedures and the practitioner's right of appeal to the Judicial Committee of the GMC; but unlike the GMC Disciplinary Committee hearings, those involved in the FPC procedures are not held in public nor is the errant practitioner named (see, Merrison Report,1975, para.323). In terms of the action taken by the FPC, there is an element of compensation for the patient built into the system; but it is not possible to tell from the official statistics to what extent this power is used.

Perhaps the most fundamental defect of the system is that it excludes many of the grievances which patients have. It had been primarily intended to ensure that GPs were fulfilling their contractual obligations to firstly local insurance committees, then to Executive Councils, and since 1974 to Family Practitioner Committees - patient complaints being one means by which this might be attested. It was a system which dealt with complaints from patients, but was not specifically a system designed to deal with those complaints (Klein,1973,pp.106,135,136).

Despite the limited impact of the Franks Committee on

42

procedures in the NHS, the Council on Tribunals subsequently took an interest in the workings of this complaints machinery, perhaps partly in response to the growing catalogue of criticism. The 1968 Green Paper on reorganising the NHS proposed to leave the system unchanged (Ministry of Health,1968,para.34). The Council on Tribunal's Annual Report for 1968 devoted four pages to responding to the Green Paper, stating that they attached great importance to 'the inclusion of improved arrangements for dealing with disputes and inquiring into complaints in any proposals for re-organising the administrative structure of the NHS' (Council on Tribunals, 1969, p.10). It was the Council's view that substantial changes were required in the working of Service Committees, and in particular that there should be a limited number of legally qualified chairmen, that the time-limits for making complaints should be extended and that the present 'complicated and cumbersome' procedures and Regulations should be revised and simplified (see, Council on Tribunals, 1969, pp.11,12).

However when the White Paper on NHS organization was published in 1972 it included the statement that 'the statutory disciplinary arrangements ... will be unchanged' (DHSS, 1972, para.68). The Council's Annual Report for 1972/3 commented as follows:

> In the context of the legislation on the reorganization of the NHS we have sought and obtained assurance from the DHSS that, when the necessary work of revising subordinate legislation (and in particular Service Committee regulations) was undertaken, account would be taken of the views the Council have more than once expressed in recent years.

The Council also noted, perhaps more in hope than anticipation, that 'we have presented the Department with a comprehensive memorandum of proposals for change in those arrangements' (Council on Tribunals,1974,para.65). The Council was disappointed to find that when the new regulations were eventually submitted to them by the DHSS they

> did not introduce any fundamental changes in the machinery for handling complaints...furthermore, we were concerned to learn from the Department that a decision appeared already to have been taken, without further consultation and full explanation, not to pursue further any of the changes we had proposed...we also felt that a new proposal in the regulations, aimed at excluding entirely representation by a legally qualified person, whether paid or unpaid, at service committee hearings, called for an explanation. (Council on Tribunals, 1975, para.51)

These proposals for the reform of the Service Committees were subsequently said to be causing concern among family doctors - their concern being that the outcome of such changes would be to tilt the balance in favour of patients and place the Committee on a more formal and judicial footing, which they did not favour (Slack,1977,p.173). The 1977/78 Annual Report of the

Council recorded that they had continued their discussions with the DHSS on proposals to modify the procedures relating to the making of complaints about family practitioner services. It concluded as follows:

> We understand that Ministers have now completed their consideration of these submissions, and that the next step will be for the Department to negotiate the resulting proposals with the contracting professions and the Family Practitioner Committees. (Council on Tribunals,1978,para. 6.11)

The next steps concerned the organizational status of the FPC within the NHS. The publication of the DHSS Consultative Paper 'Patients First' (DHSS, 1979) recommended that the FPCs retain their existing status despite other organizational changes in the NHS (the replacement of Area Health Authorities by a larger number of smaller District Health Authorities). The subsequent 1982 reorganization confirmed the new autonomous status of FPCs and in some respects returned the administration of family practitioner services to the position occupied by Executive Councils in the pre-1974 NHS structure. In 1985, the FPCs were reconstituted as health authorities in their own right and were made responsible for planning and developing primary care services and expected to assess need, identify priorities, and inform the public (Campling, 1987, p.244).

In its discussion paper on primary health care, published in April 1986, the Government eventually responded to the long-standing criticisms made by the Council on Tribunals, conceding that 'the statutory procedure is complicated and often time consuming' and that there was 'room for improvement in the arrangements' (Secretary of State for Social Services, 1986, p.17). These improvements included the suggestions that all FPCs should offer some kind of informal conciliation procedure, that patients should not be obliged to put their complaints in writing, that the existing time limits for making complaints may be too restrictive, and that there should be an examination of the most appropriate means of representing patients interests before Service Committees. There was also some recognition of those complaints that are excluded from the system because they are not matters of contractual liability and cannot be investigated under the present FPC procedures. It was suggested that such matters could be brought within the scope of the informal conciliation procedures (see, Secretary of State for Social Services, 1986, ,pp.16-18).

Within four months the Government had produced a Consultation Document on the Complaints Investigation Procedures (DHSS,1986b) which proposed that in future, all FPCs should operate an informal conciliation procedure; accept and act on oral complaints; ensure that there should be an equal number of professional and lay members at the beginning of any Service Committee hearing; and that the time limits for making complaints should be extended (8 weeks to 13 weeks). The Document also suggested that it should be possible to accept complaints lodged with the District or Regional Health Authority and that FPC Service Committees should be enabled to

44

recruit members from outside the FPC boundary. It was also clear that the Government was unhappy with the strict interpretation of the regulations that led some FPCs to exclude Community Health Council (CHC) secretaries as patient representatives in the FPC proceedings. Although it was also apparent that there was a commitment to keep proceedings as informal as possible the Document invited suggestions for ways in which the interests of parties might be most appropriately represented before Service Committees (see, DHSS, 1986b, p.5). Finally views were also invited on whether the powers to summon witnesses and obtain documents currently allowed at the later appeal stage (Stage 11, see pp.40/1) should be vested in Service Committees, and whether the FPCs should take decisions where at present they make recommendations to the Secretary of State (Stage 6, see, pp.40/1).

Five months later the Social Services Committee voiced its support for the Government's intention to make the complaints procedure simpler, more accessible and more effective and recommended that the Government consider whether useful lessons could be learned from the hospital complaints procedure (see, Social Services Committee, 1987). The Committee were subsequently thanked for their support when the Government published its White Paper on improving primary health care, one chapter of which was devoted to 'Complaints about the Family Practitioner Services' (see, Secretary of State for Social Services, 1987, Ch.8). In the White Paper the Government committed itself to the previous recommendations and suggestions on oral complaints, complaints received by DHAs or RHAs, informal conciliation, time limits, and professional and lay membership for the beginning of hearings. The problem of impartial treatment by small FPCs is to be resolved by transferring cases to another FPC for investigation and the regulations are to be clarified to ensure that a party to a Service Committee hearing can be represented by the secretary of the local representative committee or by the secretary of the CHC. Finally the Government propose to streamline the system to make FPCs responsible for determining the outcome of complaints, and the action to be taken, such decisions being final, except in the event of an appeal to the Secretary of State or in cases where the FPC believes a withholding of fees (above a certain level) to be desirable (see, Secretary of State for Social Services, pp.45-46).

Conclusions Two things seem clear from recent developments. Firstly, there has been some tangible and positive response from the Government to the long-standing criticisms of the FPC procedures for dealing with complaints; and the Government's proposals will go some way to meet some of these criticisms. Aspects of the FPC model have been emerging, and will now be enforced by the Government (eg procedures for conciliation and representation by CHC staff), which have much to commend them.

Secondly, the situation does remain unsatisfactory in a number of respects. For example, the procedures are to be simplified with most decisions to be within the ambit of the FPC with limited referral to the Secretary of State; but the fourteen-stage proceedings represented above (see,pp.40/1) are still a possibility. Most significantly we are to continue with a situation where many complaints which are not about matters of contractual liability cannot be investigated through the FPC procedures. The White Paper merely states that 'complaints of this kind may be followed up by the administrator of the FPC (Secretary of State for Social Services, 1987, para.8.2).

This whole process of reform has focused on the FPC procedures in isolation from those for dealing with complaints about the NHS hospital services - a separation that may continue to make sense from the professional or administrative perspective, but which is likely to make much less sense to the NHS patient. This continued separation attracted critical comment from the Association of Community Health Councils on the same day as the Consultation Document (DHSS, 1986b) was published. The Association criticised the number of different procedures for dealing with complaints about the NHS and concluded that 'each procedure seems to have been created more in the interests of the providers of health services than the users...for an ordinary member of the public the situation is confusing' (see, The Guardian, 4 August,1986).

The other major element in this 'confusing system' - the separate system for dealing with complaints about hospital services - developed following the establishment of the NHS in 1948; and it is this further channel for complaints to which we now turn.

Hospital services

The number of written complaints about the care given in NHS hospitals is not great in relation to the total number of patients treated. The DHSS reported a figure of 15,000 per year for England in 1983, of which about 6500 involved criticism of the clinical services (DHSS, 1983). This is equivalent to about one complaint for every 900 patients treated (see, Scott, 1985, p.70).

The establishment of the NHS did not lead either to an extension of the NHI GP complaints machinery to cover hospitals and hospital personnel, nor to the establishment of a parallel but similar system of complaints procedures for the hospital sector. The former is explicable in terms of the 'tripartite' administrative structure and, more significantly, the 'independent contractor' status of GPs. The latter may also relate to the GP's self-employment status, in so far as that explains some of the peculiarities of the system outlined in the previous section.

That does not explain why the hospitals ended up with an essentially 'domestic' system by which, for example, the disciplinary control of staff was exercised entirely by the hospital authority itself in accordance with procedures laid down in official memoranda. Thus whereas the general practitioner had the right of appeal to the Secretary of State against all the various disciplinary actions which may be taken against him through the complaints system for general practitioner services; in hospital medical practice, only the consultant had the right of appeal to the Secretary of State against dismissal by a hospital authority.

The Davies Committee Report on Hospital Complaints procedure found that the two basic characteristics of the then current system of investigating patients' complaints were firstly that it was almost entirely informal - that is complaints were investigated by those who were responsible , however remotely, for providing the service subject to complaint; and secondly,that hospital authorities were free to decide upon their own procedures for investigating complaints, subject only to guidance on broad principles issued by the Central Department (see,DHSS,1973,pp.9-10).

If a complainant was not satisfied with this internal investigation the Committee found that there was 'no clear guidance' as to what should be done (DHSS, 1973, p.8). All the DHSS appeared to do in such cases was to satisfy itself, so far as it could on the basis of a written report from the hospital authority, that the complaint had been properly investigated by the authority or its officers. As the Committee concluded, this procedure did not amount to 'an independent review of the way in which the hospital authority has investigated a complaint' (DHSS, 1973, p.9). Thus those enquiries under legally qualified Chairmen set up by hospital boards to investigate very serious complaints or events were the only external element present in the hospital complaints procedure. However as the Committee observed, few such enquiries were appointed and there was 'inadequate guidance on the setting up and conduct of ... (such) ... independent Inquiries' (DHSS, 1973, p.8).

Patients could utilise these complaints procedures independently of both court action and a referral to the GMC, but the Davies Committee observed that the attitude to such complaints was too often 'sue or shut up' and that hospital authorities had been inhibited by the fear that complaints machinery may be used solely as a means of obtaining evidence to support civil legal proceedings and that their bias had therefore been towards the non-disclosure of relevant information (see, DHSS, 1973, p.6 & p.48).

Other aspects of the hospital complaints procedures that did not emerge as satisfactory from the review undertaken by the Davies Committee included considerable variation in the way hospital authorities dealt with suggestions and complaints, and serious gaps in the information provided to patients, relatives and friends on how to make complaints or suggestions (see, DHSS, 1973, Ch.9). Perhaps inevitably in these circumstances they also discovered, as Klein had with his study of the situation with regard to general practitioners, a 'submerged iceberg' of complaints and suggestions (see, DHSS, 1973, Ch.5). A review of the Ely, Farleigh and Whittingham enquiries also indicated the inadequacies of established machinery and its inability to deal with complaints as they arose (see, DHSS, 1973, Ch.4).

The Davies Committee proposed to tackle the major problems of variability and the lack of external checks by the creation of a Code of Practice, laid down by the Central Department, which should be uniformly applied to all health authorities in all hospitals they administer and by the establishment of independent Investigating Panels (see, DHSS, 1973, Ch.6, pp.51-56). The latter were to consist of both professionally qualified and lay members under a legally qualified chairman to be used to assist in the investigation of any complaint that could be the subject of litigation but where the complainant does not intend to start legal proceedings.

The Committee considered that the proposed Investigating Panels, combined with the establishment of the Health Service Commissioner and the continuing powers of the central department and the hospital authorities to set up independent enquiries would create sufficiently independent and external checks on what would in future be a standard internal complaints procedure (see, DHSS, 1973, Ch.9). However the proposed Panels were not greeted with approval by the medical profession (Watkin, 1978, p.123).

In February 1976 the Secretary of State announced acceptance of the main recommendation of the Davies Committee that health authorities should have a written and uniform code for handling patients complaints. She also suggested that such a code should cover complaints outside hospital as well as those within and it should be subject to detailed consultation with health service authorities. A draft consultative document proposing the new code of practice for investigating complaints against hospitals and hospital doctors was subsequently sent to health authorities in June 1976. The Council on Tribunals commented that the Draft Code contained no statutory guidance of a procedural nature and noted that we have 'reaffirmed in the Department our view that there should be statutory rules for these inquiries' (Council on Tribunals, 1977, para.101). The Health Service Commissioner also confirmed the necessity for a code of practice to be established (Health Service Commissioner, 1976). In February 1976, the Secretary of State also announced that she had asked the House of Commons Select Committee on the Parliamentary Commissioner for Administration to consider the Davies Committee recommendation that investigation panels in each health service region should look into complaints that might lead to litigation.

The conclusions of the Committee were slightly more broad-ranging. They found the Draft Code for dealing with hospital complaints to be much too complicated and recommended that it should be substantially simplified. They also concluded that health authorities should not set up their own 'ad hoc' enquiries given that they are potentially defendants in any action for damages brought by a complainant. With regard to their specific brief they did not support the introduction of Investigating Panels since rather than simplifying the procedures, they would represent another channel of investigation and might anyway be seen by complainants as not sufficiently independent of management. Instead the Select Committee recommended that all cases not resolved by using a uniform but simple code of practice for handling complaints and subsequent referral to the District Administrator or another senior officer (in cases where the complainant remained unsatisfied), should be referrable to the Health Service Commissioner (see, Chapter Four) and that in this arrangement complaints concerning clinical judgement, as well as other complaints, would be referred to the Commissioner (Select Committee on the Parliamentary Commissioner for Administration,

1978). The annual meeting of BMA representatives (July 1978) were said to have 'united in angry opposition to a suggestion that the authority of the Health Service Commissioner should be extended to the consideration of complaints from patients which involve clinical judgement' (Slack, 1979, p.86).

The Government did not implement the recommendations of the Select Committee and instead requested that the profession should devise an acceptable procedure which resulted in the proposals of the Joint Consultants Committee of the BMA (see, British Medical Journal, 22 November,1980). These proposals - described as 'unbelievably complicated' by one consultant (see, Harris, 1981) - formed the basis of discussions between the DHSS and representatives of the Joint Consultative Committee. The outcome, in 1981, was a DHSS Circular (HC81/5) which introduced a new three stage procedure on 1 September,1981 (see, Figure 3.2).

The first stage of this procedure followed previous guidance by encouraging the local resolution of complaints (see, Figure 3.2, 1); and the vast majority of cases involving criticism of clinical services continued to be dealt with at this stage (see, Parliamentary Commissioner for Administration Committee, 1985, p.90). The second and third stages incorporated new measures for those cases where the complainant was dissatisfied with the outcome of the first stage.

The second stage provided for the Consultant concerned to refer and discuss the complaint with the Regional Medical Officer (RMO), with the possibility of a further meeting between the Consultant and the complainant (see, Figure 3.2, 2). If the complainant has not done so before, the complaint has now to be made in writing. In the first twenty-eight months of operation, 21% of the cases referred were dealt with at this stage (see, The Parliamentary Commissioner for Administration Committee, 1985, p.90).

(1) THE FIRST STAGE: The local resolution of complaints
    (referral to Consultant in charge of patient; discussion
    between complainant and Consultant)

(2) THE SECOND STAGE : Referral & discussion with RMO

(3) THE THIRD STAGE : Referral to two independent Consultants
    (The Assessors)

(4) Assessors Report to RMO

(5) RMO produces summary of Assessors Report

(6) Letter from District General Manager to complainant based
    on RMO's summary

Figure 3.2   Stages in dealing with clinical complaints about
             the hospital service in the NHS

If one of the parties remains dissatisfied, the procedure moves to its third and final stage which involves a professional review by two independent consultants in active practice in the specialty. These consultants are nominated by the Joint Consultants Committee (see, Figure 3.2, 3). This takes the form of a consultation with the complainant, including a review of the case records and a discussion with the staff concerned in the patient's care. However the RMO has the discretion to decide that a complaint is not suitable for an independent professional review because it is not sufficiently serious. The DHSS guidance indicates that this final stage is intended to deal with complaints of a substantial nature - but 'substantial' is not defined; although it is stated that the procedure should not be used for cases where more formal action by the health authority or through the courts is thought likely or appropriate. With regard to the latter, an undertaking is required from the complainant that s/he will not proceed to litigation if the complaint is to continue to be dealt with under the complaints procedure. It should be noted that the independent Consultants will not provide a detailed report for the complainant; they report their conclusions to the RMO and may comment on matters requiring action by the health authority (see, Figure 3.2 - 4,5,6). Finally, the procedures provide for a complainant to be accompanied by a relative or personal friend. It has been accepted that a Community Health Council officer or member may act in this capacity (see, Scott, 1985, p.72).

The English Regional Medical Officers reviewed the new procedure for the first twenty-eight months of its operation (see, Scott, 1985). In this period the Regional Medical Officers received 392 complaints of which 303 were accepted but 59 had to be referred back to Districts for the completion of the first stage. By the end of the period under review, a decision had been taken to embark upon the third stage of the enquiry in 114 (37.6%) of the cases. In 94 of these cases the inquiry had been completed; in 11 of these cases the Assessors identified clinical practices with which they disagreed, most of which resulted from organizational rather than personal failures; some were based upon differences of opinion (for further details, see, Scott, 1985).

These new procedures, although widely seen as an improvement on what went before, have continued to attract criticisms. These include the time involved in seeing the complainant from the original lodging of the complaint; the time taken by RMOs to investigate a complaint; variations between Regions and Districts in both the number of complaints received and the time taken to deal with them; the cost to the administration of the health authorities (DHA & RHA); and the uncertainty of the outcome (see, for example, Rosenthal, 1987, pp.252-53). It is still suggested that the procedures seem 'more designed to protect the profession than secure the interests of the patient...(with)...the entire investigation being kept within the profession' (Martin,1984). The Regional Medical Officers' recommendations included the need for

a greater sense of urgency and more diligence... in investigating complaints when first received at District level...that the procedure should require District General Managers to submit a report on the action which has been

50

taken on the Assessor's recommendations...(and on)...the
need (for RMOS) to make use of additional professional
assistance in their work. (see, Scott, 1985, p.72)

The process of reform has continued with the Hospital
Complaints Procedure Act, 1985, which obliges health
authorities in England and Wales and Health Boards in Scotland
to set up a complaints procedure for hospital patients and to
draw such a procedure to the attention of patients. The
Minister had the duty under Section 17 of the NHS Act,1977 to
issue directions for the implementation of this legislation and
in June 1986 the DHSS issued a Consultation Paper on the 1985
Act (DHSS, 1986a). It outlined a suggested procedure for
dealing with complaints including the following key elements:

a designated officer to receive and investigate written
complaints made by or on behalf of patients;

a report of the investigation to be provided to the
complainant and anyone implicated in the complaint;

health authorities to monitor the handling of complaints and
assess their wider implications for service delivery; and

publicity for the procedure in admission booklets, leaflets
and notices.

The designated officer proposed in the Consultation Paper
would be the recipient of all formal complaints about both
clinical and non-clinical matters, but s/he would not
investigate the former, which would continue to be handled in
the manner set out in Figure 3.2 (see, p.49). In addition
complaints about community health services do not fall within
the scope of the procedures to be laid down under the 1985 Act,
although it was proposed in the Consultative Paper that similar
procedures should be adopted, including the clinical complaints
procedures (see, DHSS, 1986a, p.6). Finally it was suggested
for consideration that health authorities should provide an
avenue of appeal for complainants or staff dissatisfied with
the outcome of the designated officer's investigation. But this
would only apply to non-clinical matters and appeal would not
be outside the authority but to one or more members of the
health authority.
The Hospital Complaints Procedure Act 1985 (Commencement)
Order 1989 subsequently required that the Act should come into
force in July 1989 (see SI 1989 1191 <c.39>). The associated
DHSS Circular followed closely the recommendations included in
the 1986 Consultation Paper. As anticipated the effect of the
1985 Act has been to create a statutory complaints procedure
which follows the broad structure of that set out in the 1981
Circular (see, Capstick, 1985, p.32). There is no doubt that
the 1981 Circular and 1985 legislation can be seen as:

a step forward from the 'shut up or sue' attitude which
previously prevailed, but it is notable that professional
opposition was able to overcome the recommendations of the

Davies Committee (and) the Select Committee on the Parliamentary Commissioner. (Martin, 1984)

Conclusions There is little doubt that the publication of the Davies Report and subsequent discussions have gradually yielded what are widely perceived as improvements to the system for dealing with complaints about hospital services in the NHS. There can also be little doubt that there remains a perception that the system could be further improved.

Whilst the hospital complaints system has never been as complex as that developed for the family practitioner services, it can be quite time-consuming. Yet for its costs in time to both complainant and key personnel (RMOs) its outcome remains strangely uncertain - hence the RMOs recommendation that District General Managers be required to submit reports on action following the independent professional review. There is no evidence that the RMOs have been unfair in their discretionary power to prevent a complaint proceeding to Stage Three (see, Figure 3.2, p.49); but it is an important discretion and one upon which the Government have issued singularly limited guidance. It is also the case that the original observation in the Davies Report still carries some weight - that to a considerable extent complaints are investigated by those who are responsible, however remotely, for providing the service subject to complaint. This also applies to those who might be recipients of an appeal about the procedures as they effect complaints about non-clinical matters.

Whilst it has with some justification been claimed that the procedures established in 1981 have provided patients for the first time with a non-legal avenue for pursuing complaints about the exercise of clinical judgement by hospital doctors (see, DHSS, 1986a), the non-legal avenue is only opened by seeming to shut off the legal avenue. These very understandable concerns of the health authorities concerning litigation may clearly pose dilemmas for complainants after Stage Two of the procedures (see, Figure 3.2, p.49). In particular it might be claimed that it is only when the matter has been referred to independent professional review that a complainant may consider that litigation is indeed an appropriate course of action, despite making the required statement that such a course of action is not proposed (see, Capstick, 1985, p.22).

Conclusions

One issue in this review of avenues for redress outside the courts (ie GMC and NHS procedures) is their relationship to the older remedy of 'going to law'. What perhaps is most perplexing to the patient, is the variation in these relationships, especially between the different NHS complaints systems.

We have noted the evolution of the relationship between the GMC and the NHS, including both the unclear status of this relationship and the differences in the GMC's links with the family practitioner and hospital complaints systems. There are the parallel, but different, systems that the NHS has maintained, based on its partial inheritance of the system devised for the National Health Insurance scheme. There is the further distinction between clinical and non-clinical matters. The GMC and family practitioner complaints system may deal with both. But in the hospital complaints system there is a distinction. Our description has focused on the system for dealing with clinical matters. Non-clinical matters, which can include very serious complaints about the standard of nursing care, are dealt with by a different system in which the health authority's main response is envisaged as a letter of explanation (see, Capstick, 1985, p.16). The proposals in the 1988 Circular give the two systems a common starting point with the designated officers, but beyond the initial reference to those individuals two separate pathways are retained. There is the added complication that the 1985 Act does not apply to the community health services.

Thus from 1912 onwards the NHI/NHS patient has had three avenues available for pursuing a case of medical negligence (the courts, the GMC and the NHI/NHS complaints system), each of which only partially and variably precludes the opportunity of taking advantage of the others. Given the hazards of litigation, developments outside the courts for dealing with complaints and concerns about medical care must be welcomed. But the welcome afforded to the systems described in this chapter must be qualified by a concern about the rather complex system that has been established. In particular, it is ironical that the arguments put forward to justify the establishment of the National Health Service laid stress on gains for efficiency and for social justice; commentators have subsequently found the systems for dealing with complaints about the Service to be neither efficient nor just. Furthermore, the efforts of the last twenty years to unify the organizational structure of the NHS have contributed nothing to any unification of even the first and most informal stages of dealing with complaints about the Service.

Finally we might note that our historical review of the NHS systems has revealed another paradox. That the hospital complaints procedure emerged from the Davies Report looking even less satisfactory on a number of counts than the system for dealing with complaints about general practitioner services – but it had been the latter that had borne the brunt of the critical comment for the first twenty years or so of the NHS's existence. That imbalance of critical comment has been redressed somewhat in the second twenty years of the NHS. The second twenty years of the NHS has also witnessed other developments which have added further dimensions to the Service's complaints procedures. It is to these developments that we now turn our attention.

4 Changes, criteria and conclusions

Changes

The advent of the National Health Service meant that aggrieved patients now had four possible avenues of complaint - the courts, the GMC, the Family Practitioner Committee complaints procedures and the hospital complaints procedure. For twenty years little was done either to remedy any of their alleged defects, or to complement them by alternative avenues for dealing with complaints or monitoring practice. However from 1968 onwards a number of changes took place which need to be examined as part of any comprehensive review of medical negligence and medical accidents. The prelude to the first of these innovations involved a dramatic increase in the use of an existing but seemingly dormant power to establish special inquiries into serious allegations (beginning with Ely Hospital). For more than a decade these enquiries became a regular and almost accepted part of the health service complaints scene (see, Martin, 1984); the attention that now focused on conditions in long-stay institutions prompted the establishment of the Hospital Advisory Service.

(a) The Hospital/Health Advisory Service

The Hospital Advisory Service (HAS) was established in 1969. Its functions were laid down as follows:

by constructive criticism and by propagating good practices and new ideas, to help to improve the management of patient care in individual hospitals and in the hospital services as a whole;

to advise the Secretary of State for Social Services about conditions in hospitals in England and the Secretary of State for Wales about conditions in hospitals in Wales.

In April 1987 the Hospital Advisory Service became the Health Advisory Service and broadened its concern from hospital services (especially long-stay hospitals) to all health services. In so far as the HAS's brief excluded matters of individual clinical judgement it has never been conceived as an avenue through which individual patients might pursue cases of medical negligence. However it is clearly a potentially significant institution in relation to the general issue of maintaining good standards of medical care and its future role is a relevant issue in any discussion about the possibilities for reform.

(b) The Health Service Commissioner

When the Parliamentary Commissioner Bill was being debated in Parliament in 1966 and 1967, one feature which attracted criticism was the provision of Schedule 3, which excluded National Health Service hospitals from scrutiny by the Parliamentary Commissioner (Stacey, 1978, p.126). Arguments were advanced in favour of providing an 'ombudsman' for the NHS in the influential book 'Sans Everything' (see, Abel-Smith in Robb (ed), 1967) and by the Select Committee on the Parliamentary Commissioner (Select Committee Report on the Parliamentary Commissioner for Administration, 1968). In the same month as the latter appeared (July 1968) the First Green Paper on NHS reorganization was published and included suggestions that 'consideration might be given to bringing the relevant activities of the Area Health Boards within the ambit of the Parliamentary Commissioner' or alternatively a 'Health Commissioner' might be established. However such a Commissioner would not

intervene in an issue such as an allegation of negligence which could more properly be pursued in the courts', nor would the Commissioner be 'concerned with clinical matters to a greater degree than an 'ad hoc' board of enquiry set up under existing arrangements by a hospital authority. (Ministry of Health, 1968, paras.79 & 80)

The Second Green Paper stated that consultation with professional and other interests was continuing about the proposal for a Health Service Commissioner (DHSS,1970). The appointment of a Health Service Commissioner with 'the widest possible powers' was one of the recommendations of the Report of the Farleigh Hospital Committee of Enquiry (DHSS,1971,p.29). Despite the generally critical attitude of the doctors' organizations (see,Stacey,p.177), the setting up of a Health

Service Commissioner (HSC) was announced by the Government in February 1972 and the Secretary of State's statement was published as Appendix II of the White Paper on NHS reorganization. The Commissioner would

> consider only those complaints made by or on behalf of patients which have already been made to the responsible authorities and not been resolved to the complainant's satisfaction...nor will he investigate the actions of general medical and dental practitioners, pharmacists, ophthalmic medical practitioners and opticians, all of whom are not employees of the Health Service but are under contract with it.

It had also been decided that

> the Commissioner should be precluded from investigating any action taken in the course of diagnosis, treatment or clinical care of the individual patient which, in the Commissioner's opinion, was taken solely in the exercise of clinical judgement.

Finally, like the Parliamentary Commissioner, the HSC would not look into complaints when the complainant has, or had, a right of appeal to a tribunal or a remedy by way of proceedings in a court of law, unless it is unreasonable to expect the complainant to resort to or have resorted to it (DHSS, 1972, pp.55-56). The proposals were implemented in the NHS Reorganization Act 1973 and the HSC began to receive complaints in October 1973.

In many respects the HSC has similar powers to the Parliamentary Commissioner although he does have a wider frame of reference in that the HSC can investigate failure of a relevant body to provide a service which it was a function of the body to provide (see,NHS Reorganization Act, 1973, Section 34). Stacey lists the main advantages of the HSC's kind of investigation as including:

> ready access to relevant information;

> less cumbersome and protracted than tribunal proceedings:

> the ability to follow up cases to see if there has been a change in unsatisfactory practices;

> uniformity of standards; and

> the accountability of the HSC through his reports and the Select Committee system (see, Stacey, 1978, p.184).

An important issue regarding the HSC is the extent to which his role is restricted by the limitations placed on his ability to investigate complaints. Indeed, the Davies Committee had expressed some concern about the exclusion where a remedy at law was available given their finding about the inhibiting effect that the fear of possible litigation has on the investigation of hospital complaints. They also expressed the hope that the HSC would 'not take a narrow view' with regard to the exclusion placed upon matters of clinical judgement (DHSS, 1973, paras.10.6, 10.7 and 10.10). This exclusion was the subject of prolonged argument before the office was established and it is this limitation, along with the exclusion of EC/FPC complaints procedures, that constitute the other significant restriction on the work of the HSC. Reviewing the first ten years of HSC's work, the Commissioner commented that

> the large majority of those who seek an investigation are denied even the limited satisfaction of knowing that an Ombudsman has considered their complaints, because their complaints do not fall within my jurisdiction. (Health Service Commissioner, 1984, p.2)

This circumstance applied to 67% of complaints received during these first ten years (see, Health Service Commissioner, 1984, p.10). Commenting further on 'these restrictions on my jurisdiction', the Commissioner noted that

> by far the most important numerically - and this has been consistent over the ten years - is the exclusion of action taken in connection with the diagnosis of illness or the care or treatment of a patient and which, in the opinion of the Commissioner, was taken solely in consequence of the exercise of clinical judgement. (Health Service Commissioner, 1984 , p.2, para.5; see also the 'Reasons for rejections' table, p.44, Appendix B)

Despite the recommendations of the Select Committee on the Parliamentary Commissioner that the HSC's activities should be less severely restricted, we remain in a situation where the HSC's inability to investigate matters concerning clinical judgement may force complainants towards the courts and the 'hazards of litigation'. We are also left with some seemingly strange anomalies by which questions of clinical judgement can be investigated by the Parliamentary Commissioner if it concerns patients in hospitals directly controlled by central government (ie special hospitals and Ministry of Defence hospitals); and the HSC can investigate complaints about all other aspects of the work of FPCs (including the removal of patients from doctors' lists) and their informal conciliation procedures. Indeed Stacey's conclusion was that 'the Ombudsman's method of investigation is highly appropriate for examining complaints about procedural defects in administrative tribunals'. He concluded that if the HSC is to be fully effective, the bars against his investigation into matters of clinical judgement and the FPC complaints procedures should be removed (Stacey, 1978, p.190).

(c) Community Health Councils

> the councils are not generally streamlined, powerful, efficient and assertive organizations.
> Levitt,1980,pp.27-28

> CHCs have not been well organised in their role in assisting patients to complain.
> Stacey,1978,pp.193-94

> Only a minority of the general public knows of ..(their)... existence.
> Levitt, 1980, p.46

The idea of Community Health Councils (CHCs) seems to have emerged as a result of the decision to reorganise the NHS outside of local government in 1974 and therefore to rely on non-representative health authorities to administer the service (see, Levitt, 1976, pp.9-19). They obviously owe something to the district committees proposed in the Second Green Paper on NHS reorganization (DHSS,1968,paras.53-54), emerging in their own right in the subsequent 1971 Consultative Document and 1972 White Paper, with the basic function of representing to the Area Health Authorities the interests of the public (DHSS, 1972, para.109). No mention was made of CHCs in the section of the White Paper that dealt with complaints, but elsewhere it was suggested that the CHCs might wish to provide information about the complaints machinery, and to provide a 'patients friend' where one is needed (DHSS, 1972, pp.44-45 and para.110). This latter suggestion was welcomed by the Davies Committee which noted that this was

> very important...as many complainants are not able to put forward their own case adequately and will be at considerable disadvantage if staff complained against are helped or represented by professional associations or trade unions. (DHSS, 1973, para.10.29)

Some Members of Parliament were less complementary when the House of Commons debated the relevant section (Section 9) of what was to become the National Health Service Reorganization Act (1973). For example, Shirley Williams described CHCs as 'the strangest bunch of administrative eunuchs any department has yet foisted on the House,a seraglio of useless and emasculated bodies' (Brown, 1979 ,p.29). Whilst this may appear a somewhat harsh and hasty judgement, it was obvious that considerable uncertainty surrounded the CHCs and the roles they were to perform. It was not even clear which 'community' the CHCs were intended to represent - users of the NHS, vulnerable groups needing special protection, or the local population-at-large (Brown,1979,p.29, Klein & Lewis,1976,p.17)

The first major attempt to eliminate some of the uncertainty that attached to the role of the CHCs was the DHSS Circular on Community Health Councils issued in January 1974. Paragraph 9 of the appendix to this circular dealt with the role of CHCs in relation to complaints and stated that:

the investigation of complaints will be a matter for the
health authorities and its staff or (where appropriate) for
the Health Commissioner or Service Committee but Community
Health Councils will be able, without prejudging the merits
of individual complaints or seeking out the facts, to give
advice, on request, on how and where to lodge a complaint
and to act as a 'patients friend' when needed. (DHSS
Circular HRC (74)4)

The wording of this particular communication was variously
described as 'somewhat tortuous', 'extremely ambiguous' and
'confusing' and Klein and Lewis found a number of CHCs to be
'puzzled as to how to interpret ... the circular' (Klein &
Lewis,1976,p.143 and Levitt,1980,p.18 & 27).
 The rights and responsibilities of CHCs have been
subsequently amended, most significantly in the 1975 Circular
(HSC (IS) 194-Democracy in the NHS) which announced the final
decisions on the suggestions put forward in the consultative
paper - 'Democracy in the NHS: membership of health
authorities' - that the new Labour Government had produced in
May 1974 (DHSS,May 1974). However nothing had been produced
which sought to clarify the CHC's role in relation to
complaints.
 The Secretary of State (David Ennals) tried to extend the
CHC's right of attendance to FPC meetings, but the proposal
aroused 'intense opposition and was not pressed' at the time
(Brown,1979,p.30). The Royal Commission on the NHS observed
that FPCs 'often appear to resist CHC attempts to assess family
practitioner services' and recorded that many CHCs had told the
Commission that this was their greatest stumbling block
(Merrison Report,1979,para.11.9). This was perhaps indicative
of the somewhat delicate relationship between CHCs and the
family practitioner services; a situation which has continued
(see, Allsop, 1984, p.196). However the reported establishment
of patient committees in some health centres and group
practices indicated that there was not universal hostility to
changes in this area (Merrison Report, 1979, para.11.35), and
the Royal Commission also noted that since no complaints
procedure is likely to be known or immediately understandable
to all those who might have cause to use it, there was a good
case for making the CHCs' role in complaints a more active one
(see, also Levitt,1980,pp.27-28). To this end the Commission
suggested that in the literature supplied by hospitals
informing patients of suggestions and complaints procedures,
the name and telephone number of the local CHC office should be
given prominence. They also suggested that if CHCs were to
develop their role as patients' friends that experiments be
undertaken with the sort of 'patient advocates' that exist in
the USA. There, the advocate's function was to take up problems
as they arise with the person or department responsible as
quickly and informally as possible. The suggestion was that he
or she would be based at a hospital or health centre and would
be a paid employee , part-time or full-time, of the CHC (see,
Merrison Report, para.11.25 and 11.26). The Royal Commission's
overall conclusion on the CHCs was a positive one : 'They had
been an experiment which should be supported further'

(para.11.11). At the same time the Health Service Commissioner referred to the 'increasing number of complaints (which) come to my attention because a Community Health Council has advised the complainant that I may be able to help' (Health Service Commissioner,1979,p.32), and the local CHC was one of the few bodies to emerge with credit from the Committee of Enquiry into conditions at Normansfield Hospital (see, Slack, 1979, pp. 388-89).

It was somewhat surprising, in the light of the Royal Commission's generally positive conclusion on CHCs, that the Government's first major response should include the suggestion that the CHCs might be unnecessary following a further reorganization of the NHS (see, DHSS, 1979, para.26). This threat to the whole future of the CHCs was lifted in the subsequent DHSS circular on the new reorganization (DHSS Health/Local Authority Circular HC(80)8/LAC (80)3,Health Service Development,Structure and Management,July 1980,Paragraph 21.).

The current complexity of complaints procedures makes the CHC's assistance of potential benefit to complainants; but their value remains limited by the continuing lack of clarity concerning their role - with a variety of interpretations being placed on the DHSS advice by different CHCs. Whether they have the resources to make a more effective contribution in helping individuals with their complaints is obviously another important issue (see, DHSS,1981). The Royal Commission warned that it would only be possible for CHCs to undertake a more active role as advisor and 'friend' in complaints procedures at the expense of other important aspects of their work, unless more resources were made available (Merrison Report, 1979, para.11.25). Lack of clarity about the role of CHCs in acting as advocates for individual patients, allied to their lack of resources, has resulted in limited public awareness of their existence.

Even if there were more widespread recognition of the CHCs as providers of information on complainants, and the CHCs had sufficient resources to provide 'patient advocates' along the lines suggested by the Royal Commission, would there be a conflict between representing the interests of those individuals who have a complaint and representing the interests of the 'other communities' (eg all NHS users) ? (see, Levitt, 1980,p.53). The effectiveness of a number of roles that have been given to CHCs will continue to rest - despite the rights they have been given - on the maintenance of reasonably good relations with other institutions in the NHS - the District Health Authorities, the Regional Health Authorities, the FPCs, and NHS management. Whilst the provision of information and basic guidance about complaints procedures may not endanger such relations, it is possible that a more effective playing of the 'patient advocate' role may do so.

The situation is therefore one in which the current complexity of complaints procedures makes any assistance afforded by CHCs as likely to be beneficial to the complainant. In the absence of any effective alternatives to assist and advise patients with complaints the continued existence of CHCs in the NHS must be considered a gain.

(d) <u>The National Development Group and Team</u>

The National Development Group for the Mentally Handicapped (NDG) was set up in February 1975 by the Secretary of State for Social Services to advise her on mental handicap policy and on its implementation. The NDG was described as having a 'considerable measure of independence' by the Secretary of State (see, NDG, 1976, p.iii). The Development Team for the Mentally Handicapped (NDT) was complementary to the NDG and intended to provide advice to field authorities about the planning and operation of services. The NDT was also independent of the relevant Government department, as far as its operation was concerned.

The NDG was disbanded in 1980, but the NDT continues to operate. As with the HAS, neither body was directly concerned with individual complaints about service provision. However such independent bodies scrutinising current policies and practices may be seen as an important element in controlling and maintaining the standard of service and minimising the risks of cases of medical negligence and medical accident.

(e) <u>Mental Health Commission</u>

The Mental Health Act,1959 had inaugurated a new deal for mentally ill and mentally handicapped patients. But experience showed that the new deal had its own defects, and the Mental Health (Amendment) Bill in 1981 sought to remedy some of these. As a result of considerable attention which the new Bill then received, it was substantially changed before it was passed in 1982 and was subsequently superseded by the Mental Health Act, 1983. The principal changes introduced by the 1983 Act were designed to improve the right of patients or potential patients and facilitate their proper treatment. These changes included the establishment of the Mental Health Act Commission (MHAC). The Commission was set up on the 1 September 1983 and started its statutory duties on the 30 September,1983.

The tasks assigned to the Commission under the Act include:

protecting the interests of detained patients by visiting and interviewing them in hospital and mental nursing homes; investigating complaints by and about detained patients; and keeping under review the way in which powers and duties under the Act are carried out;

arranging for the provision of 'second opinions' by appointed doctors (and in special cases, also by lay people), where the Act requires such opinions to be obtained before treatment is given to detained patients (or,in special cases, to informal patients as well); and carrying out 'reviews' of such treatments at later stages, where second opinions have been given;

drafting a Code of Practice for the guidance of doctors and other professionals in relation to the admission of patients under the Act and the proper treatment of both detained and informal patients;

reviewing any decision made at a special hospital to withhold a postal packet or its contents, if a review is applied for.

The Commission consists of a Chairman and 91 other members. The services of all Commissioners are part-time. The Commissioners are drawn from different professional backgrounds, but also include lay members. All have a particular knowledge or interest in one or more fields of the mental health service. The Commission had

no existing pattern or framework for performing those tasks which it had to undertake one month after being set up...that framework has been developed empirically as the Commission has gathered collective experience. (MHAC, 1985, p.6)

The result was to give each of three Regions a degree of autonomy in order to respond to variations in practices and to employ local knowledge. The effect is to make the Commission a large multi-disciplinary team, operating through progressively smaller teams of similar multi-disciplinary origin.

The MHAC's jurisdiction to investigate complaints is governed by Section 120(1)(b) of the Mental Health Act. Although its function in investigating complaints has many similarities to that of the HSC, there are also differences, and the MHAC is itself subject to investigation by the HSC. This is likely to concern principally the propriety and efficiency of procedures rather than the merits of cases into which the Commission has inquired. The MHAC's role in dealing with complaints has been interpreted as providing a second stage where a complainant is not satisfied after taking an issue through the hospital's own complaints procedure. Although this is the normal route which the MHAC initially recommends, a primary investigative function is not ruled out in some cases.

By contrast with statutory complaints procedures, the Commission's function does not necessarily end when a complaint is upheld or dismissed. The MHAC can then pursue another role, of overseeing the exercise of powers and duties under the Act. From the particular complaint the process can move on to look at broader issues which may affect staff and patients at a hospital or group of hospitals. However whilst it was thought by many individuals that the MHAC was 'endowed with 'teeth'..in fact it does not bite very much' (MHAC,1985,p.34). Unlike the HSC or the Scottish Mental Welfare Commission, the MHAC has no judicial powers, for example to compel attendance of witnesses or to deal with a failure to co-operate by way of contempt of court. However it can exert pressure; as the Commission itself notes

the results may be slower and less dramatic, but there are signs that they may be effective. The mishandling of an individual situation may be irretrievable, but intervention may prevent it happening again to that or any other patient...the emphasis often shifts from the actual

complaint to a review of the way in which a hospital or
unit is observing the spirit of the Act.
(MHAC,1985.p.34,p.35)

For such activity the MHAC considered that a 'formalised
procedure would be out of place' (MHAC, 1985, p.36).
   The MHAC has categorised the complaints it has received as
set out in Table 4.1. From this it can be seen that two
categories (medical treatment and professional care) constitute
almost 40% of all complaints, with medical treatment forming
the largest single category.

Table 4.1
Categories of complaint received by MHAC
(figures are expressed as percentages)

	1983-1985	1985-1987
Medical treatment	13.39%	15.3%
Professional care:	24.81%	23.8%
(a)Medical care & services	8.93%	8.5%
(b)Nursing care & services	8.56%	9.3%
(c)Other professional care & services	7.32%	6.0%
Leave,parole,transfer,other absences from hospital		
	11.78%	10.9%
Offences against the person	8.31%	10.4%
Deprivation of liberty	8.06%	8.3%
Mental Health Review Tribunal matters	7.94%	11.4%
Domestic care,living arrangements & privacy		
	5.33%	4.6%
Administration	5.08%	5.0%
Financial benefits and property	4.71%	4.8%
DHSS,Home Office & other govt.departments	3.72%	1.6%
Social,recreational,educational matters	3.47%	1.0%
Local authority services/functions	1.48%	1.6%
Complaints about the MHAC	0.74%	0.5%
Ethnic,cultural,religious matters	0.62%	0.2%
Family matters	0.49%	0.6%
Total number of complaints received	1549	1231

Sources: MHAC,1985,First Biennial Report of the Mental Health
Act Commission,1983-1985, HMSO.
         : MHAC,1987,Second Biennial Report of the Mental Health
Act Commission,1985-1987,HMSO.

   The Commission can receive complaints about clinical
judgement but the number and significance of such complaints is
not recorded in the MHAC Reports. Furthermore 'this type of
complaint must be made by a patient who either is or has been
detained'. Areas of clinical judgement are excluded for other
patients (see,MHAS,1987,p.13 & p.18). In addition before the
Commission can investigate 'the managers of the hospital must
have been given the opportunity to carry out their own

investigation' (MHAC,1987)

The MHAC is a relatively recent innovation and to date has produced only two reports on its work. These reports suggest that the Commissioners are still working out their future role and at present attempting to agree a Draft Code of Practice with the DHSS. It is therefore too early to judge their role in individual patient complaints. It is however reasonably obvious that the MHAC are dealing with some of the most difficult questions that can arise between patients, professionals and the state, especially because of the civil liberty issues involved in compulsory detention for treatment. There is also complex, but possibly unavoidable, overlap with the work of the HSC.

Criteria

There was a time when the only recourse available to complainants was to pursue a case of medical negligence through the courts. But the court system is adversarial, it may be cumbersome, slow and expensive, and it is concerned with relatively narrow concepts such as those of negligence and damages. However the last 132 years has seen the development of institutions which provide alternative means of dealing with cases of medical negligence - the GMC (1858), the EC/FPC complaints system (1912), NHS hospital complaints procedures (1948), the HSC (1973) and the CHCs (1974). This raises the whole issue of the relative merits of these different systems.

Knowledge and accessibility

Do complainants know of the existence of the various systems ? Whilst occasional banner headlines in the popular press may create an awareness of the existence of the GMC, they may be less aware of the NHS hospital and FPC procedures. Whether CHCs could or should be expected to fulfil an information-providing role is one issue, although it immediately raises another of whether people know of the existence of CHCs. One virtue the courts may possess is that their presence may be more widely known than the more recent developments.

The right to assistance

What assistance do complainants have? Do they need and can they obtain specialist professional advice? Although dependent on the complainant's means and the 'reasonableness' of the case, legal aid is available for the 'oldest remedy - going to law'. Such aid is not available for the GMC and NHS systems.

The right to complain

How satisfactory are the various mechanisms for filtering out the frivolous or vexatious complaints? Can we be satisfied that all the complaints taken out of the system do indeed fall into these categories ? Is there scope for informal pressures, including the informal conciliatory procedures, making the right to complain less obviously a right than it is supposed to be. Similarly, the continuing variation in hospital complaints procedures found by the Davies Committee and the RMO's Report may equally effect the visibility and appearance of what is intended to be a right to complain.

The operation of the machinery

It was the opinion of the Council on Tribunals that
> whatever mechanisms are chosen should be as simple as possible, and that a person wishing to lodge a complaint should not be deterred by complicated or obscure procedures or by the hearing of his complaint in conditions which he might find intimidating (Council on Tribunals, 1977, para.3.19).

The Council was expressing its opinion in relation to the proposed reform of hospital complaints procedures but it had, along with many other observers, already made critical comments on the FPC system because of its general complexity and the sort of procedures used.

The most obvious simplification - a complaints procedure for NHS complaints, rather than separate ones for hospitals and GPs never appears to get on the agenda for reform. Its apparent non-acceptability as a policy option may be affected by a number of factors including the continuing administrative separation of FPCs; the closely related independent contractor status of GPs; and the non-liability of the NHS for the torts of the self-employed GPs. The 1987 White Paper (Secretary of State for Social Services, 1987) concentrates on a streamlining of the current FPC system. Welcome though this might be, it could be seen as an opportunity missed to take on board the common issues that unite complaints across the entire National Health Service.

A further significant issue concerns lay involvement in the various procedures we have reviewed. For example, should there be increased lay membership of the GMC ? (see, Robinson, 1988, pp.36-37). There is a requirement for lay involvement in the NHS family practitioner system, but this requirement is absent for the NHS hospital complaints system.

What sort of redress - for individuals ?

Only the Courts offer the complainant a real possibility of being compensated for an act of medical negligence. Given the possibly disastrous effects of and the non-returnability of bad medical care, the issue of compensation is worthy of consideration. If the Courts are little used for pursuing cases of medical negligence, should one of the other systems have more extensive powers to compensate complainants?

What sort of service - for the community ?

Klein noted that 'if the consumer of professional services could be relied upon to complain whenever he gets a poor service, a complaints machinery would be an effective way of protecting him against poor quality. If however,he cannot be relied upon to do this...then a complaints machinery, whatever its uses, can only make a very partial contribution to maintaining standards'. He further observed , with regard to the EC/FPC system that 'as a source of information for pinpointing those doctors who are failing to deliver the goods as specified in their contract, the complaints machinery is little better than spinning a roulette wheel' (Klein, 1973, p.156 and p.138). Whilst improving accessibility of the complaints machinery might increase its effectiveness as a form of 'general quality control', the implication seems clear; we need to develop alternative systems to take on this role. The HAS, NDT and MHAC provide useful models, in which some sort of compromise is sought between professional autonomy and public accountability.

Conclusions

> The second floor was lighter and cleaner, but that didn't mean it was clean and light.
> Raymond Chandler, <u>Farewell My Lovely</u>, Penguin, 1949, p.190

There remains something of a paradox in all these developments; namely that in terms of most of the criteria necessary to give confidence in all the systems, the courts emerge as the most satisfactory means of dealing with cases of medical negligence! This is because complainants have potential access to legal aid, the possibility of gaining compensation for any loss they have suffered, a degree of equity between defendant and plaintiff, and justice is seen to be done as the proceedings are held in public.

Suggesting that the Courts emerge quite favourably in a comparison of the various alternative means of seeking redress is not to suggest that the courts represent the 'best we can do'. Rather it is a stark reminder of the manifold limitations and inadequacies of many aspects of the alternatives to the Courts that have been developed since 1858. This clearly does not provide us with the basis for being either satisfied with court proceedings or content to leave our current complex of complaints systems unchanged.

Firstly and quite significantly, whatever the rank ordering of these alternative avenues for pursuing a complaint, for the man or woman in the Clapham Health Centre perhaps the most striking thing about the systems is that they present a rather complicated and fragmented picture. The existence of so many alternatives and the rather complex and at times bewildering relationship between them does not make for a generally satisfactory situation.

Secondly, whatever their virtues court proceedings do not resolve many cases of alleged medical negligence. It is indeed likely that there is yet another 'submerged iceberg', this time of potential litigation that could be revealed by, for example, extending the availability of legal aid or lawyers working on a contingency-fee basis. In so far as the courts (or court-like procedures) are appropriate for resolving certain sorts of cases, we should certainly seek to make those procedures more accessible than the present system of litigation.

Thirdly, there has been more than one comment to the effect that 'the vast majority of complainants - despite what some powerful doctors urge - do not want to go to law, they are not out for money'. For this majority of complainants we certainly need something more than access to the courts which obviously brings us back to the adequacy of the alternatives to the courts. And of course the courts only fare well in our evaluation because of the quite marked limitations of the various alternative avenues that have been established.

Finally, the 'cleaner and lighter' elements of the British system may anyway fade somewhat by comparison with what has been developed in other countries. For example, Rosenthal (1987) is extremely critical of the British system by comparison with the Swedish system. She concludes that:

> Britain has an extensive collection of complaints mechanisms, increased use of the courts, and no integrated system for information feedback for medical injury prevention. The British public is increasingly discontented. Sweden on other hand has developed an interrelated system that is compensatory, regulatory and preventive .... it stands in striking contrast to the current British and American tort systems which are inequitable, inefficient, costly and arbitrary to both consumer and physician. The tort systems compensate (perhaps over-compensate) a few badly-injured patients, but make no distinction between malocurrence (error) and malpractice. It is not clear that it deters bad medical practice and it has little prospect for prevention.

She further suggests that a 'no-fault' approach could 'forestall a burgeoning of its (Britain's) own inequitable tort system'.

There are many problems with resolving issues concerning medical negligence through the courts. But court proceedings have a number of virtues that have not always been incorporated in the extensive alternative collection of complaints mechanisms that have grown up alongside them. This is not a case for continuing to rely on court proceedings in the way we have in the past. However it does suggest that we should not readily deny access to the court, until we are satisfied that their advantages have been firmly lodged in one or other of the alternative avenues for complaint and redress. And in pursuit of such reforms we should neither ignore the political context in which such reforms will have to take place nor be unaware of the ethical complexities and conflicts inherent in constructing a fair system of control and compensation. With these considerations in mind we will examine the current agenda for reform - the range of proposals for changing our responses to the issue of medical negligence.

5 Agendas for reform

> For this is not the liberty which we can hope, that no
> grievance ever should arise in the Commonwealth - that let
> no man in this world expect; but when complaints are freely
> heard, deeply considered, and speedily reformed, then is
> the utmost bound of civil liberty attained that wise men
> look for.
> John Milton, <u>Areopagitica</u>, November,1644 (quoted in the
> Health Service Commissioner's Annual Report 1983-84)

This is an interesting time to be reviewing reforms. A range
of suggested changes have been advocated over the past few
years - we have had Private Members Bills referring to both
the GMC and hospital complaints procedures and we have had
government proposals for reforming the complaints systems for
hospital and family practitioner services. There also seems to
be increasing interest in the idea of no-fault compensation -
a system by which financial compensation would be payable to
victims of medical mishaps regardless of their cause and with
no requirement to identify a negligent act (see, for example,
BMA, 1987).

The central question remains. Can we devise a system that
recognises the widely held view that compensation is both fair
and appropriate for victims of medical negligence and at the
same time give consideration to the needs of the victims of
other negligent acts, including non-medical professional
negligence, and of both medical and non-medical accidents?

Our hopes and expectations of administrative and legal
structures for dealing with public claims against private

professionals or public corporations is that the structure of redress is so designed as to make the redress as smooth and as stress-free as possible. Quite a broad spectrum of opinion is agreed that Britain's 'extensive collection of complaints mechanisms' in the health field does not live up to these expectations. However the range of suggested reforms indicate there is less agreement about how the defects of this 'collection of complaints mechanisms' should be remedied.

One reason why the court proceedings have proved increasingly problematic is due to a sort of 'system overload'; although not with individual cases - we may well have a 'submerged iceberg' of medical accidents and medical negligence. The overload is in the goals we are attempting to pursue through court proceedings. This would accord with previous critical comments on the alternatives to court proceedings (see, for example, Bell, 1969, Street, 1968, and Klein, 1973, p.145).

What goals do we wish to pursue? We can identify the following as the most important aims, although the list is not intended to be exhaustive.

Definition of good practice

Promotion of good practice

Prevention of bad practice

Identification and investigation of bad practice

Elimination of bad practice

Compensation for those who have received bad practice

The picture is further confused by the presence of both 'bad practitioners' (for which an individualistic approach is required to identify and possibly remove the unsafe practitioner) and 'bad practices' (for which a generalised approach is necessary). So the prevention, investigation and elimination functions will need to employ both individualised and generalised approaches.

There is then the related problem of medical error and medical accidents. Understandably attention has focused on compensation for medical accidents - a clear parallel to the focus in many discussions on court proceedings in negligence cases. But given that the effects of error and accident can be every bit as profound as those of medical negligence, there is a case for considering not merely how we should seek to compensate, but also to prevent accidents and to identify and eliminate possible sources of error in the system.

Are we expecting certain procedures/institutions (perhaps most obviously court proceedings) to perform too wide a range of related, but disparate functions? The illustrative examples in Figure 5.1 (see, p.70) suggest that this may be the case; they also suggest that our existing institutions focus more on certain of the goals. We have a system that appears to emphasise a reactive approach to negligent practices and negligent practitioners.

These are serious issues and we may well justify their being the primary focus. But given their significance should not more attention be paid to the issues of promotion and prevention; and elimination and compensation. Similarly the lack of concern with 'compensation for error' seems to be paralleled by a lack of concern with the prevention, identification and elimination of sources of error.

One conclusion is that all these goals are worth pursuing, but they cannot all be achieved in the context of one system and one set of procedures. What we may need is a range of institutions and procedures to address these different issues.

	Courts	GMC	FPC	HOSPS	HAS	HSC	CHC
DEFINITION good practice	■	■			■		
PROMOTION good practice		■			■		
PREVENTION: the bad practitioner		■					
PREVENTION bad practice							
IDENTIFICATION: the bad practitioner	■	■	■				
IDENTIFICATION: bad practice	■					■	■
ELIMINATION: the bad practitioner		■					
ELIMINATION bad practice	■			■			
COMPENSATION for bad practice	■						
PREVENT: accidents/errors							
IDENTIFY: sources of error and accident							
ELIMINATE sources of error and accidents							
COMPENSATE accidents/errors							

Figure 5.1 Institutions and aims

But if that is the case we think it must be conceded that what we have evolved in the UK is a set of institutions and procedures which duplicate some and not other functions in a far from logical or systematic manner. Furthermore, as we have already indicated there is inevitable confusion concerning the way the institutions operate alongside one another - one can pursue several avenues of redress at the same time, but on the other hand certain actions may preclude others. And different criteria are being employed (eg. balance of probabilities, beyond reasonable doubt) by different institutions.

This is the crucial point; can we seek to integrate all procedures in such a way that specialised arrangements are devised to match the most common causes of 'failure' – meaning accident, negligence, error, deviant conduct – any or all of which may result in damage to a dependant person whose trust has been placed in a professional approach? One answer may be that we should retain, as now, a range of institutions; but that their relations one with one another needs to be much more clearly defined and more readily comprehensible than the bewildering range we have evolved over the past 132 years. We should go for system simplicity rather than system complexity. But at the same time we need to recognise that there are complex issues to be resolved for which there will not always be cheap and simple solutions available. We would support the well-established maxim that 'expensive justice is better than cheap injustice' (Brougham)

Through what means might our various goals be carried out? Below we have identified a number of approaches, some of which clearly parallel existing institutions and procedures. Our argument is not that these are clear-cut, competing alternatives. These approaches clearly overlap with, and can complement one another. However they do indicate the range of approaches upon which our system – our 'range of institutions' – must be based.

The judicial approach would involve opportunities for questioning, complaining about, and reviewing procedures using the court-like conventions with which we are familiar; this would include the courts, the tribunals and the special enquiries that can be established within the NHS.

The professional self-governing approach would include standards set for recruitment, education, training, and competence to practice; it assumes that the service-ideal is imbued in individual practitioners; it seeks to exercise control through maintaining a register of safe, competent practitioners and excluding those that do not continue to meet the appropriate criteria. This approach is obviously represented by the GMC.

The bureaucratic/managerial approach would include the setting of standards and guidelines, the control of services, and the setting and enforcement of various rules and regulations. It may be that efforts to introduce clinical budgeting and performance indicators in a health service with general managers represents the best example of such an approach.

The democratic approach would include systems of public/community/consumer representation. In the absence of directly elected members of RHA and DHAs and the widely accepted limitations of Ministerial accountability through Parliament, it may be that for the moment the CHCs represent our best example of this approach.

The conciliatory approach would provide for discussion,

71

exchange of views, settlement of differences in an informal manner with limited rules and guidelines about what is said, who is present, and so on. The current provisions of the FPC and hospital complaints machinery include elements of conciliation.

The consumerist approach would provide for a degree of consumer control. The most obvious form is the market mechanism or some replication of that (voucher systems). A degree of consumer control may be achievable through other means – for example, consumer representation and participation which clearly takes us back to the democratic approach. This illustrates our earlier comment that these are not neat self-contained categories.

It may be possible to combine elements of the professional and bureaucratic approaches. This could be by ensuring that professionals occupy key managerial/bureaucratic positions and thereby imbue the organizational controls with a sense of what is professionally correct. Alternatively, independent organizations could be established that can review practices and are either staffed by professionals (inspectorates, HAS) or can seek appropriate professional advice (HSC and appropriate clinical assistance where necessary)

Similarly the professional self-governing procedures will be likely to use a judicial approach in deciding whether particular practitioners should be struck off the list of approved practitioners. So in terms of actual institutions/procedures we will find both the existing system and any reformed system employing more than one of these approaches to perform more than one of our basic functions. Indeed the range of goals outlined above (see Figure 5.1) do indicate it will probably be necessary to use a variety of approaches.

What is particularly apparent is that much of the existing system uses the judicial approach (see Figure 5.2). This we may regard as a parallel to our previous observation that the focus has been on the identification of 'bad practice' and the bad practitioner'. It may well be that the judicial approach is

	Courts	GMC	FPC	Hosp	HAS	HSC	CHC
JUDICIAL	■	■	■	■			
PROFESSIONAL self-governing		■			■		
BUREAUCRATIC managerial				■	■	■	
DEMOCRATIC							■
CONCILIATORY				■	■		■
CONSUMERIST							■

Figure 5.2 Institutions and approaches

particularly important in and relevant to those tasks. But this does lead to the suggestion that the present system is biased in the sense of focusing on one particular approach (the judicial approach) to pursue a particular set of goals (identification of 'bad practice' and the 'bad practitioner). If we are to address seriously our range of desirable and complementary goals it may be more appropriate to make increasing use of the other approaches we have identified.

Before reviewing the various agendas for reform, we must return to some of the themes of our opening chapter. There we commented on the enduring flexibility of the legal concept of medical negligence. But have court proceedings in cases of negligence and the other avenues for seeking redress for grievances, accommodated changes in the pattern of health care delivery?   Have our systems of control and accountability adapted to changing circumstances?   One feature of modern health services is teamwork. None of the texts refer to cases where the complaint concerns both GP and hospital services, but the complainant in such circumstances would be faced with a most confusing situation. Why does a complaint against a health authority have to be pursued through a separate channel? Why does 'double jeopardy' concern the authorities responsible for the hospital services, but not those responsible for the family practitioner services? Why does dissatisfaction with action taken allow for an appeal to the HSC in one case, but not the other?   Is sufficient account taken of teamwork in modern health care - teamwork between medical practitioners in both hospital and community settings, and between the medical, nursing and other para-medical professions. Indeed the pressure - for economic and medical reasons - to make optimum use of in-patient facilities means that more and more hospital-based health care is part of a 'package' of health care that involves community-based medical and nursing colleagues.

Continuing support for policies of 'community care' further complicates the picture. Here the 'care' that is provided may be a combination of medical, nursing and social care from multi-disciplinary teams. For example, we can consider the position of a recently discharged mental illness hospital patient who receives a domiciliary visit from a consultant, whilst remaining under the care of a general practitioner with support from a community psychiatric nurse and some involvement from a social worker. The care and support may be planned by this multi-disciplinary team and the patient may be dissatisfied with what they have done as a team. The patient could complain about the GP through the system for complaints about family practitioner services; about the consultant through the system for dealing with complaints about clinical matters in the hospital services; about the community psychiatric nurse through the system for dealing with complaints about non-clinical matters in the community health services; and about the social worker to the local authority Social Services Departments. This is without considering different systems of professional control (GMC, UKCC) or the possible role of the courts.

This does not render obsolete the concept of bringing some sort of complaint against an individual practitioner. We can continue to anticipate circumstances in which a complaint is appropriately directed at an individual member of the sort of team described above. But there would surely be other circumstances in which a complaint was most appropriately directed at a practice, or set of practices, that were in a very real sense a team responsibility. This does suggest that there should be opportunities for aggrieved patients or their relatives to complain about the 'treatment' and/or 'care' provided by health care agencies, with perhaps a diminishing emphasis on directing complaints at individual practitioners.

In Chapter One we also noted that the evolution of Britain's system of health care, and by implication its related 'collection of complaints mechanisms', could be understood in terms of political expediency. We may also understand disputes about how it should be reformed in terms of the different political interests involved. Can any reform encompass the concerns of administrators, lawyers, politicians, treasurers and medical professionals? Administrators may be looking for smooth, known, certain, rule-based, recordable, decision-making arrangements. Lawyers and politicians may be looking for a system that is based on precedent, case-law, legislative debate, with minor or few political costs. Treasury officials and health service treasurers are looking for a system which is not financially open-ended, which may be self-funding and buoyant without becoming a burden on the Treasury or the tax-payer. Is it possible to devise a system which will meet these wide-ranging and possibly conflicting demands on the system? What is politically feasible given these potentially conflicting interests?

An ideal model of reform would represent the ethics of the categorical imperative, and above all respect for the patient in the system, it would be rooted in such criteria as knowledge and accessibility, the right to complain, the right to assistance, and the quality of the service. But will an ideal model ever be realised? Although there is a strong ethical case for known, certain, understood and speedy and just systems of compensation, there is no necessary connection between the ethics of idealism and the practicalities of administration; especially where that idealism is based upon lay or consumer beliefs rather than professional knowledge.

A feasible reform model might emphasise the professional and bureaucratic approaches as being the most practical. Practicality in this sense means that methods to ensure that professionals occupy key managerial positions in the NHS would have the effect of imbuing the organizational procedures for investigating complaints with the sense of what is professionally correct in defined circumstances; and secondly by giving the opportunity of establishing independent professionally staffed arrangements that can review practices and at the same time can ask the appropriate professional questions and therefore make judgements about appropriate clinical matters where necessary.

It might be argued that professionals and consumers should

be looking for the same ideal outcome - a risk-free doctor/patient relationship in which if 'things go wrong' (error,accident,negligence) liability is met without punitive sanctions on the professional (being sued, public reputation despoiled, loss of professional confidence) and avoidance of additional stress, incapacity, and psychological feelings of 'spoiled identity' for the consumer/patient. But the interests of professionals, consumers and the wider community may not always be in accord; they may, for example, place a different value on the criteria (e.g. knowledge, accessibility) we introduced at the end of Chapter Four. It would certainly oversimplify matters to suggest that those criteria were the only ones by which we might judge both the current system, and proposals for reform, which returns us to the theme of the complex web of ethical assumptions and conflicts which surround the development and delivery of modern health care (see,Chapter One).

So in reading the contemporary agenda for reform we have a range of questions to be kept in view. Questions concerning the goals we wish to set for our system of complaints procedures; the approaches by which we might pursue those goals; the current and probable future changes in the nature of health-care delivery; the political context and the range of political interests that may need to be accommodated in order to get acceptable and workable reforms; and finally the range of ethical issues that are central to some of the dilemmas which our existing system has sought to resolve. With these considerations in mind we will examine the current agenda for reform - a range of proposals which would change our responses to the issue of medical negligence.

Agendas for reform

We begin with an agenda of general reforms which are concerned with more than either one part of or all of our 'extensive collection of complaints mechanisms' but which nonetheless would have some bearing on issues relating to medical negligence. We then review the agenda of specific reforms which looks at some of the suggestions for reforming one or more of the institutions we have focused on in Chapters Two, Three and Four. Finally we provide our own agenda for reform.

The agenda of general reforms

Proposals for specific reforms are inevitably framed in the light of both knowledge of the existing wider context, and assumptions about the potential for changes in this wider context. There are at least six categories of 'general reform' that could have a significant bearing on the sort of specific reforms that might be advocated. These are policies for open government, democratic government, legal services, services for people with disabilities, privatisation and professionalism.

A. <u>Policies for open government</u> It seems to be widely accepted

- except by those in positions of power and influence within government - that the UK could safely have a 'more open' system of government in terms of such ideas as 'freedom of information'. Moves in that direction might include or be conducive to a more 'open' health care system. This might prove helpful in retaining good doctor/patient relations. Thus whilst issues of confidentiality require some secrecy, the NHS could be encouraged to be as open as possible in terms of access to information.

There are perhaps two qualifications to be made to the 'open government' concept. Firstly, that it may be possible for progress to be made in the direction of a more 'open NHS' without a government committing itself to a broader 'open government' policy. Secondly, that an 'open government' or 'open NHS' approach may not solve problems of access to information in the private sector of health care.

B. <u>Policies for democratic government</u> It seems to be less widely accepted that the UK could become 'more democratic' by such changes as proportional representation and devolution of power to local systems of government. However it is widely accepted that democratic procedures of some sort are seen as legitimating the resulting decisions. In the context of the NHS, arguments about proportional representation and devolution need not concern us. By our conventional UK measures the NHS is 'not very democratic' which leads us to the long-standing argument that it would be beneficial to introduce more explicitly democratic controls into the NHS (eg some directly elected public representatives on health authorities). As with the case for 'openness', it is based on the assumption that we may be able to defuse some potentially adversarial situations without recourse to formal appeals machinery, if patients are satisfied that they are dealing with a 'reasonably open and democratic system of administration'. Once again there is the question of where this would leave the 'private sector' ?

C. <u>Policies for law as welfare</u> Most obviously, there is the recommendation that legal aid should apply to most tribunals which has long had the support of the Council on Tribunals (see, for example, Council on Tribunals, 1989). This view was supported by the Royal Commission on Legal Services; they also supported the principle that 'financial assistance out of public funds should be available for every individual who, without it, would suffer an undue financial burden in pursuing or defending his legal rights' (see, Benson Report, 1979, Ch.15 and p.50). These reforms taken together would make it more reasonable to assume that anyone, regardless of their circumstances, would be able to take full advantage of any judicial procedures in our present or future systems.

D. <u>Policies for disability</u> This is a very important area of potential general reform. It most obviously refers to provision of income support through schemes of 'no fault liability' and the social security system, but actually embraces a wider range of reforms and resource-allocations including housing, social work support services and of course the general adequacy of 'community care' policies. The relevant 'social policy' literature has long contained well-argued cases for the development of comprehensive policies for disability that embrace both all the necessary services (e.g. income,housing) but also all disabled people. If such comprehensive policies were in place or being earnestly pursued it may well be that questions of adequate compensation for negligence, accidents, errors, mishaps and so on would cease to be the central issue that they appear to be at present.

E. Policies for privatisation This is rather a loose label that is attached to a wide range of policies including for example both the 'contracting-out' of services by the NHS and the supplanting of the NHS by a private market in health care. In its various forms it remains a more likely general reform than A,B<C or D. However, whereas A to D could contribute to creating an environment in which patient/doctor conflicts were less frequent, some sorts of privatisation may well increase both the likelihood of litigation and other attempts to complain and criticise (see, for example, Quam,Dingwall & Fenn, 1987)

Furthermore, and regardless of any radical reforms that might be envisaged for the NHS, the private sector of health care has been growing over the past decade in terms of for example, the provident associations and private hospitals and nursing homes. We have concentrated on the position of the NHS patient - what happens to the aggrieved NHS patient? Of course for most people, most of the time, this has been and still remains the most pertinent question. But to what extent should the State seek to provide mechanisms for the aggrieved private patient? Or having 'gone private' for one's health care, is it both entirely fair and appropriate that one should 'go private' in making one's complaint (via the Courts and/or the GMC)? In answering that question how relevant is it that the state funds a substantial volume of care in private nursing homes and establishes the legal/regulatory framework within which they operate? Furthermore, those in receipt of such care are not necessarily the richer and more powerful sections of our community - one thinks of elderly people and discharged patients from mental handicap and mental illness hospitals. It is possible that current and future changes in the organization of the NHS would make these questions of increasing relevance to a wider range of patients.

Private hospital organizations are said to be considering setting up complaints procedures (see, Brazier, 1987, p.125). This would of course add yet another set of institutions to our 'extensive collection of complaints mechanisms'. Should we seek to define some sort of framework which could handle complaints and grievances about health care - regardless of the provider (state,private or voluntary organization)?

F. Policies for professionalism There have been suggestions for a Council on Professions (Klein, 1973) and for the establishment of a Code of Professional Standards of Competence

(Kennedy, 1987). It may be that the Lord Chancellor's Green Papers on the reform of the legal profession, with its strong advocacy for reforming the complaints machinery in an impartial, independent and speedy manner, may become a model for other professional bodies. The immediate response to the Lord Chancellor's papers included the Lord Chief Justice's statement that the proposed reform of the legal profession (not just the complaints machinery against solicitors) was 'one of the most sinister documents ever to have emanated from government' (The Guardian, February 16,1989). This reaction to a reforming Lord Chancellor and subsequent reports that the Bar Council had raised £350,000 towards a target of £1 million against the Green Paper using Saatchi and Saatchi to organise the campaign does not augur well for the reform of other professional bodies whose procedures might be the subject of legal review, when clients complain.

The agenda of specific reforms

These proposals focus primarily on one part of 'the system' we have been looking at. To review these proposals we will repeat our previous chronological approach (see,Chapters 2,3,4).

A. The hazards of litigation There are two main responses to the problems of existing court proceedings. One strand involves attempts to remedy perceived defects whilst retaining the basis of a fault-based system. For example, it has been suggested that we could simplify pre-trial procedures and introduce a system of arbitration (Carson,1988). There is the idea of 'the structured settlement' (see,Allen,1988) in which damages are paid by means of periodic payments rather than in a one-off lump sum. Such settlements follow agreement by the parties to the claim and are, it has been claimed, 'enormously flexible' (Allen,1988). Whilst we retain a system which involves settlements by the courts this could overcome some of the recognised limitations of the lump-sum method.

We have already noted that at present it is only the Courts that appear to offer the complainant a real possibility of being compensated for an act of medical negligence. Given the possibly disastrous effects of and the non-returnability of bad medical care, the issue of compensation is worthy of consideration. If the Courts are in the end little used for pursuing cases of medical negligence, should there be an alternative system for compensating complainants? This suggestion raises a further and quite central dilemma concerning our responses to medical negligence and medical accidents. We can see that both raise questions of compensation. Should we not compensate for losses incurred by cases of both medical negligence and medical accident? Clearly a key criticism of tort is that the better compensation goes to those who suffer negligence, but the needs of those who suffer accidents is equally great. This leads us in the direction of no-fault systems of compensation - the notion of removing certain areas from the purview of fault-based litigation and replacing them with systems of no-fault compensation.

This is the other strand of responses to the problems of court proceedings; and it is one which has attracted growing support (see, for examples, BMA,1987, Dingwall,Fenn and Harris,1988). The Pearson Commission, whilst taking a generally cautious line on this question, did advocate no-fault compensation for road accident victims. In Sweden there is a no-fault system covering medical accidents which has attracted strong support (see,for example, Rosenthal,1987, and Brahams, 1988). The no-fault idea has been introduced most extensively in New Zealand in 1974 following the recommendations of the Woodhouse Commission (1967) and legislation in 1972. Under this sort of scheme it is intended that 'damages are by definition related to needs not deeds' (McLean,1985). It is clear that such schemes (Sweden and New Zealand) can resolve an inequity between the accident-victim and the negligence-victim - an inequity that seems all the more profound given the difficulties of distinguishing clearly between misjudgments and negligence. But no-fault systems can pose other ethical dilemmas. For example:

Should the concept of negligence exclude certain professional groups - does no-fault mean the concept would continue to apply to the plumber and window-cleaner but not to the doctor or nurse?

Should we compensate medical accidents more effectively than other accidents which may befall individuals or than other disabilities and handicaps from which individuals may suffer?

It is this non-universal nature of some no-fault schemes that has attracted criticism, along with new dividing lines and exclusions that can be identified. In New Zealand sickness is excluded, and 'while the distinction between accident and sickness may in some cases be clear, in others it may be highly problematic' (McLean,1985). The Pearson Commission voiced some of these concerns when it noted that the New Zealand Accident Compensation Commission seemed concerned to avoid slipping down the slippery slope and compensating illness or death every time medical treatment fails (Pearson Report, 1978, para.1354). This means that in many cases the claimant is left once again with recourse to the Common Law.

Similar criticisms can be directed at the more narrowly defined Swedish system which covers only medical injuries, so the medical/non-medical dimension becomes significant. This scheme also excludes those natural and probable consequences of justified medical intervention. Once again the Pearson Commission was critical on this point, noting that less than 50% of claims were admitted as valid (Pearson Report, 1978, paras.1355-58).

Is there any sense in which we might argue that the victims of negligence do deserve or expect some additional form of compensation? Is there a case for additional compensation for those who have suffered a loss which they would not have suffered if they had been treated by a prudent,competent practitioner? Do we resolve the traditional issues of consent, choice and compliance in such a way that it inevitably leads to an expectation of compensation if things go wrong?

This leads us to consider the complex set of interrelationships between a wide range of issues which forms the context of our discussion of medical negligence. In relation to compensation for victims of accidents or negligence, can we make any assumptions about the future provision for people with physical and mental disabilities through social security programmes and other state welfare provision? This is clearly an important question because contrary to Lord Lawton's comment in <u>Whitehouse v Jordan</u>, the community does care for the victims of medical mishaps and has done so for some considerable time. Throughout the industrial world systems of means-tested public assistance have evolved to cover all negligence and accident victims, indeed all victims of any sort of disability. What Lord Lawton's comment reflects is an opinion, that may well be widely supported, that faced with the circumstances of the sort of tragic case to which he was referring, the community's response is inadequate. But this argument can be applied with equal strength to those whose needs are similar, but were not caused by a medical mishap.

There is a clear 'feasibility' argument for advocating reforms that do not assume radical change in our existing social security programmes. However in so doing we must recognise the potential political significance of such a course of action. Victims of medical mishap do attract public attention and public sympathy. To ameliorate their problems in isolation from the needs of other disabled people, may severely weaken the political viability of more fundamental reforms that would benefit a more substantial group of currently disadvantaged individuals. However it would fit in with an established pattern of development in which there seems to be a growing recognition for particular groups of people of the limitations of a continued reliance on the two most long-established systems of compensation - fault-based litigation and means-tested public assistance. The result is the movement of certain categories of need into some system of no-fault compensation, most significantly through social insurance/social security programmes. We then have to live with the consequences of new divisions and continuing exclusions (see Figure 5.3, p.81).

The central question remains. Can we devise a system that recognises the widely held view that compensation is both fair and appropriate for victims of medical negligence and at the same time give consideration to the needs of the victims of other negligent acts, including non-medical professional negligence, and of both medical and non-medical accidents?

B. <u>Outside the courts</u> The theme most often taken up in relation to the GMC is whether matters regarding professional competence and clinical judgement should be given over to a strengthened GMC (see, for example, Klein, 1973). The Merrison Committee was of the opinion that the GMC's role should remain restricted to dealing 'in relation to matters which are sufficiently serious to raise a question of a doctor's

FROM
fault-based litigation   and   means-tested public assistance
for negligence   for negligence, accidents and
inc.medical negligence   all causes of disability

TO

no fault compensation
for
industrial disability (UK,1906)
war disability
road accident disability (Pearson,1978)
medical accident (Sweden)
all accidents (New Zealand)

exclusions from non-universal no-fault compensation?
          unavoidable consequences of necessary treatment
                                                    (Sweden)
          sickness (New Zealand)
          non-essential medical intervention (Sweden)
          emergency medical intervention (Sweden)
          unavoidable side-effects of drug therapy (Sweden)

Figure 5.3 Alternative responses to the consequences of
           disability

continued right to practice' (Merrison Report, 1975, para.233)
and advocates of the idea have conceded that it would involve
a surrender of lay power; although this might be minimised by
increasing lay participation in the GMC (see, for example,
Rosenthal, 1987, and Robinson,1988).
   Concern about the limitations on the present role of the GMC
has led to a Private Members Bill which sought to enable the
GMC to consider a lesser charge of 'unacceptable conduct' in
relation to the GMC's minimum penalty which makes registration
conditional on compliance with some action, such as working
under supervision (Robinson, 1988,p.5, Brazier,1987,p.17). We
should add that there is no evidence that the GMC wishes to see
its role extended.
   Both the FPC and hospital complaints procedures have been
extensively criticised and governments have responded in ways
which go some way towards recognising the case made by the
critics. However reservations remain about the effectiveness
and fairness of the improved procedures. The FPC system still
concerns itself primarily with breaches of contract by
independent contractors, there is limited lay involvement in
the hospital system, and the case for some unified system of
NHS complaints procedures remains unanswered. Suggestions for
further reform as separate or unified procedures tend to
involve extending the role of the HSC and CHCs.

C. The newer institutions The longest-standing and perhaps
most significant recommendation for reform in this area is that
the brief of the HSC be extended to cover issues of clinical

81

judgement which has been a matter of concern since the Commissioner was established (see, Chapter Four) and has been consistently advocated for many years. The other almost as long-running suggestion has been the establishment of a more significant and more clearly defined role for CHCs in relation to representing the aggrieved consumer.

Our agenda for reform

What we have sought to do in what follows is to keep the 'whole system' in perspective. One reason for this is that it is rather easy to become involved in some of the more dramatic defects of particular parts of the 'system'. We are reminded of the invective hurled at the EC/FPC system during the 1960s in the subsequent light of the Davies Report which revealed that the hospital complaints machinery was in an even more parlous state than that for GPs.

Our proposals for reform aim to bring the various elements of this 'system' into a more logical and simpler relationship with one another. This involves seeking to eliminate some of the more obvious anomalies and confusions, creating something that is accessible and understandable to the complainant but which at the same time affords adequate protection to individual professionals where their competence becomes an issue. This must perforce involve a series of stages in any system of NHS complaints. We can seek to simplify the system but cannot, given the complex nature of the goals being pursued, offer a simple system without doing a disservice to the some of the goals we wish to pursue. In presenting our particular specific reform proposals we would like to make the following points.

We make no assumptions about the likelihood of implementing all or any of the above-mentioned general reforms.

They are based on the needs of the NHS patient and the work of the NHS doctor. We have excluded consideration of the extent to which they could or should be adapted to accommodate the grievances of the private patient and/or issues concerning other NHS professionals.

The first step - CHCs, 'patients friends' and conciliation

Where a patient or their relative is concerned about something that has happened, the first step should wherever possible be to go to the CHC. The CHC should, as the Royal Commission on the NHS suggested, seek to maintain a register of 'patients friends' who would be willing to assist in discussions about the problem. The aim at this stage should be to use some relatively informal conciliatory machinery to discuss the matter. In many cases if this is done in an open and sensitive manner many patients will be satisfied. The outcomes might be as follows:

complainant satisfied;

CHC to raise the matter with the DHA or RHA for further

informal discussions;

CHC not satisfied- refers the matter to the next stage (see below);

complainant not satisfied-refers the matter to the next stage (see below).

The aims of the first step would be to expose more of the 'submerged iceberg' of grumbles and complaints, but seek to deal with as much as possible in a friendly, open, informal manner. It should always be clear that the complaint can be taken to the next stage as quickly as the complainant wishes and the CHC/friend might advise this where it does seem to be a 'serious issue'. This stage should be clearly time-limited so that complaints can either be quickly resolved or speedily passed on to the next stage.

This first step employs elements of the democratic, consumerist and conciliatory approaches.

The second step - a NHS 'participation-model' tribunal (lay membership) This would deal with all NHS complaints; and indeed at this stage every effort should be made to consider the complaint as one against the Service (the relevant health authority or agency) rather than against individual practitioners. The notion of the 'participation-model' tribunal is not that it is totally informal, but that it should be so organised as to afford maximum opportunity for individuals to present their own case, possibly with some help from a 'patients friend'. The outcomes might be as follows:

referral to health authority for action - there should be an obligation on the health authority to formally respond within a set time period;

referral to HSC for action (especially where issues of professional competence are raised; also where the tribunal is not satisfied with the response of the health authority);

complaint dismissed (if the complainant is dissatisfied with the decision of the tribunal, they can refer the case to the office of the Health Service Commissioner).

The aims of the second step would be to seek to resolve as many issues as possible without creating a professional/patient adversarial situation or involving complainants in procedures which are not directly concerned with their complaints (eg the present FPC system)

This second step would retain elements of the Consumerist and Conciliatory approaches but would introduce a more formal, judicial approach.

An assumption What does seem certain is that the participation model tribunal would not be appropriate for cases where the technical competence of a practitioner was being called into question. The justification would follow Lord Denning's observation in <u>Cole v Hucks</u> 91960,C.A.) that

> a charge of professional negligence against a medical man was serious. It stood on a different footing to a charge of negligence against the driver of a car. The consequences were far more serious. It affected his professional status and reputation. The burden of proof was correspondingly greater as the charge was so grave, so should the proof be clear.

This suggests a more formal arrangement than would be compatible with the participation-model tribunal. It would include such characteristics as:

dispassionate examination of evidence properly adduced to the court;

regular procedures which promote an orderly and fair hearing;

the allowance of legal representation.

Whilst one expects the participation-model tribunals to aim for an orderly and fair hearing, we might anticipate an absence of legal representation for example. The implication is that more serious cases (eg alleged medical negligence) and cases where the parties remain dissatisfied after less formal procedures have been exhausted, should be dealt with in a more formal, more conventionally judicial approach requiring either a conventional Court setting or something approaching it.

<u>The third step - the offices of the HSC/HAS</u> Unresolved and serious cases could be referred to the office of the HSC, which should in future be linked to the HAS. It would take on administrative and clinical issues, although for the latter there would be a system of professional advice available. The aim would be to produce reports on the complaint as now. However we would suggest the office of the HSC could be linked with the HAS. Whilst the HAS could continue to perform its existing functions, it would now have the additional function of taking on referrals from the HSC, where the HSC considered that what was at issue was not an isolated case, or an individual practitioner, but sets of procedures or practices that needed investigation. We would also suggest the office of the HSC could be given the power to require health authorities or the Secretary of State to establish formal judicial inquiries into what were regarded as the most serious cases. We would further suggest that we would need to establish some mechanism by which the recommendations of the HSC and HAS were binding on health authorities.

Our suggestions would be that as far as possible the HSC, like the participation-model tribunals, would focus on the question of whether the patient(s) had received the sort of service they should be entitled to receive. This would not be out of line with some recent judicial pronouncements. In the Court of Appeal it was suggested in the <u>Wilsher v Essex AHA</u> case that it would be more sensible to investigate whether the health authority had organised and supervised an efficient and careful system of work, rather than to engage in an exhaustive search for some breach of standard by a clinician. That is, both the HSC and the HAS would seek to avoid an individualised approach in an attempt to leave it to the professional and employing organizations to pursue issues of individual complicity in the failure to provide a good service and whether this amounts to negligence. What the HSC might therefore do is to conclude that there is a prima facie case to answer by one or more practitioners and then refer that case to the internal disciplinary proceedings of the health authorities. We would also suggest that one of the powers of the office of the HSC could be to require health authorities to offer compensation to the complainant. Such a power would be exercised in all cases where a loss has occurred and not just where negligence is alleged and proven. The issue of what level of compensation should be made could perhaps be settled by some system of arbitration.

This third step is primarily a combination of the judicial and professional/bureaucratic approaches.

We would suggest that these three steps could provide a logical, simple system for dealing with the complaints of NHS patients, including quite serious complaints. We would hope that many complaints could be satisfactorily dealt with by the first step or second steps in the sequence. We would also hope that most aggrieved patients would be satisfied that the case had been thoroughly and fairly looked into and that justice had been done. However there are some other issues to be addressed.

Negligence, employers and the profession

In our suggestions, we have emphasised avoiding placing the individual complainant in an adversarial position with the individual professional. The office of the HSC might come to the conclusion that there is a prima facie case for considering that an individual doctor may have been negligent. But what we would suggest is that if this is the finding of the HSC, then the matter should be seen as the concern of the employing authorities and of the profession. It is therefore at this stage (after an HSC investigation) that it may be appropriate to refer matters to the internal disciplinary machinery of the health authorities and/or the GMC. We would further suggest that it should be possible for the GMC and the health authorities to come to some agreement by which an individual doctor is not assumed to answer a case in both forums at the same time. Given the burden of proof required by the GMC, it does fit logically at the end of the process.
The procedure could be:

HSC referral of individual case to health authorities (prima facie case of incompetence/negligence);

there would then follow an internal disciplinary proceeding, at which the professional would be legally represented;

the findings of these proceedings may be passed on to the GMC.

This arrangement would formalise the NHS/GMC relationship that has evolved (see, Chapter Three). Given the comments made earlier about the proposed NHS participation-model tribunals, these internal disciplinary proceedings should take a thoroughly judicial approach with adequate safeguards for the interests of the individual professional. At this point we would wish to incorporate all the advantages traditionally associated with court proceedings, even if this also involves some of the disadvantages (eg.costs,delay). However concern for individual professionals could include not conducting the proceedings in public, in which case the office of the HSC could have the remit of keeping such procedures and cases under review to ensure fairness to both professionals, and the patients who may have been the source of the case.

Courts and torts

Where would this leave the courts? At this stage we are rather reluctant to commit ourselves to the idea that it should no longer be possible to take a medical negligence case through the courts. The reasons for this are as follows.

Given that there is some relative merit in current court procedures, one would not wish to cut off that avenue until it was clear that what was in their place was better.

There may be a case for having the courts as some sort of back-up to existing and future procedures - a sort of final court of appeal (in any case any proposed system could still be subject to judicial review of some sort).

The issue of compensation - given the needs that are likely to lie outside their remit and the new problems of the dividing lines which they create (for negligence/error, read medical/non-medical or accidental/genetic), we have reservations about the proposed no-fault medical accident and no-fault accident schemes.

We have included the concept of the HSC requiring health authorities to make compensatory payments - effectively a form of no-fault compensation for any medical event that has 'gone wrong'. However once again we would not wish to cut off access to the courts until it is clear that something better is in their place. In this case the continued right of individual complainants to go to court would be a check on the compensation-payments made by the health authorities and would ensure that they did not fall too far out of line with those offered in comparable non-medical negligence cases.

Conclusions

The 'oldest remedy' for a person dissatisfied with what a doctor has done or not done has attracted a great deal of justified criticism over the years. The focus of court proceedings on the issue of medical negligence is seen as excluding a wider range of needs and concerns, including the issue of compensation for victims of medical accidents. But this criticism should not divert attention from other related institutions where there are also powerful arguments for further reform.

We have dwelt on some of the advantages of the judicial approach for certain problems. But we would also agree that the present British 'system' emphasises the judicial approach in pursuit of certain goals (identification of negligent practices and negligent practitioners) and that this includes more than just the courts. Current debates are highlighting the potential of other approaches (bureaucratic) to achieve other goals (compensation).

We would like to complement this argument by noting that there are also other approaches which have been only employed to a very limited degree so far (conciliatory and professional/bureaucratic) and other goals (prevention) which have been neglected.

Finally in pursuing these goals effectively, individual professionals are going to be the subject of complaints, criticisms, controls, evaluations and so on. We should in the light of this remember some of the traditional virtues of the judicial approach in protecting the individual rights of such professionals. Whatever other useful developments take place to pursue more effectively the neglected goals of prevention and compensation, we would argue that the judicial approach will need to be retained somewhere in the system.

Bibliography

Allen, C.K. (1956), <u>Administrative Jurisdiction</u>, Stevens, London.

Allen, D. (1988), 'A Balm for Damages', <u>The Guardian</u>, February 22, 1988.

Allsop, J. (1984), <u>Health Policy and the National Health Service</u>, Longman, London.

<u>Barnett v Chelsea and Kensington HMC</u>, 1968, 1 All E.R., pp.1068-74

Bell, K. (1969), <u>Tribunals in the Social Services</u>, Routledge, Kegan and Paul, London.

Bell, K. & others (1975), 'National Insurance Local Tribunals- A Research Study, Part II', <u>Journal of Social Policy</u>, January, 1975

Benson Report, (1979), <u>Royal Commission on Legal Services</u>, Cmnd.7648, HMSO, London.

Bewley, B. (1988), in 'Rethinking the NHS: medical complaints and medical discipline', <u>Journal of the Royal Society of Medicine</u>, July 1988, pp.424-426.

<u>Blyth v Birmingham Waterworks Co</u>, 1856, 11 Ex.781

BMA, (1987), <u>No-Fault Compensation Working Party</u>, British Medical Association, London.

<u>Bolam v Friern Barnet Hospital Management Committee</u>, 1957, 1 W.L.R. 582.586

Brahams, D. (1988), 'The Swedish Medical Insurance Scheme : The Way Ahead for the United Kingdom', <u>The Lancet</u>, January

29, 1988
Brazier, M. (1987), <u>Medicine, Patients and the Law</u>, Penguin Harmondsworth
Brown, R.G.S. (1979), <u>Reorganising the National Health Service</u>, Routledge, Kegan and Paul, London
Campling, J. (1987), Social Administration Digest, <u>Journal of Social Policy</u>
<u>Canterbury v Spence</u>, 464 F.2d 772, 780 1972
Capstick, B. (1985), <u>Patients Complaints and Litigation</u>, National Association of Health Authorities in England and Wales, Birmingham
Carson, D. (1988), 'Medical Accident Litigation', <u>Health Services Journal</u>, January 21
Cartwright Report (1988), <u>The Report of the Committee of Enquiry into Allegations Concerning the Treatment of Cervical Cancer at National Women's Hospital and into other related matters</u>, Government Printing Office, Auckland
<u>Cassidy v Minister of Health</u>, 1951, 2 K.B. 343
<u>Chandra Bhattacharya v GMC</u>, 1969, The Times
Civil Justice Review (1988), <u>Report of the Review Body on Civil Justice</u>, Cmd.394, HMSO, London
<u>Cole v Hucks</u>, 1968, C.A., The Times, 9 May 1968
Corner, T. (1985), 'Treatment and Consent: A Bad Year for Litigious Patients' in Harrison A, and Gretton,J (eds), <u>Health Care UK 1985</u>, CIFPA, London
Council on Tribunals (1965), <u>Annual Report for 1964</u>, HMSO, London
Council on Tribunals (1969), <u>Annual Report for 1969</u>, HC272, HMSO, London
Council on Tribunals (1974), <u>Annual Report for 1972/73</u>, HC82, HMSO, London
Council on Tribunals (1975), <u>Annual Report for 1973/74</u>, HC289, London
Council on Tribunals (1977), <u>Annual Report for 1975/76</u>, HC236, HMSO, London
Council on Tribunals (1978), <u>Annual Report for 1977/78</u>, HMSO, London
Council on Tribunals (1989), <u>Annual Report for 1987/88</u>, HMSO, London
<u>Crawford v Charing Cross Hospital</u>, 1953, T.L.R.
Crossman, R. (1972), <u>A Politician's Guide to Health Service Planning</u>, University of Glasgow, Glasgow
Davis, K.C. (1971), <u>Discretionary Justice : A Preliminary Enquiry</u>, University of Illinois Press, London
DHSS (1970), <u>National Health Service: The Future Structure of the National Health Service</u>, HMSO, London
DHSS (1971), <u>Report of the Farleigh Hospital Committee of Enquiry</u>, Cmnd.4683, HMSO, London
DHSS (1972), <u>National Health Reorganization</u>, HMSO, London
DHSS (1973), <u>Report of the Committee on Hospital Complaints Procedure</u> (Chairman: Sir Michael Davies), HMSO, London
DHSS (1974), <u>Democracy in the NHS: Membership of Health Authorities</u>, HMSO, London
DHSS (1979), <u>Patients First: A Consultative Paper</u>, HMSO, London
DHSS (1981), <u>Consultative Paper on the role and membership of</u>

<u>Community Health Councils</u>, DHSS, London

DHSS (1986a), <u>Consultation Document, Hospital Complaints Procedure Act, 1985</u>, DHSS, London

DHSS (1986b), <u>Consultation Document, Family Practitioner Services : Complaints Investigation Procedures</u>, DHSS, London

<u>Donoghue v Stevenson</u>, 1932, AC 562

Downie, R.S. and Calman, K.C. (1987), <u>Health Respect:Ethics in Health Care</u>, Faber and Faber, London

Eckstein, H. (1959), <u>The English Health Service: its origins, structure and achievements</u>, Oxford University Press, London

Finch, J. (1986), Letter to <u>The Times</u>, 18 September, 1986, p.15

<u>Franklin v Bristol Tramways & Carriage Co.Ltd.</u>, 1941, 1KB 255

Giesen, D (1988), <u>International Medical Malpractice Law : A Comparative Study of Civil Liability Arising from Medical Care</u>, Martinus Nijhoff, London

<u>Gerber v Pines</u>, 1933, 79 S.J.13

GMC, <u>Annual Reports</u>, General Medical Council, London

GMC (1985), <u>Professional Conduct : Fitness to Practice</u>, General Medical Council, London

<u>Gold v Essex County Council</u>, 1943, 2.All.E.R.237

Gostin, L.O. (1975), <u>A Human Condition: observation, analysis and proposals for reform,</u> Volume One, MIND, London

Griffiths, J.A.G. (1977), <u>The Politics of the Judiciary</u>, Fontana, Glasgow

Grunfeld, C. (1954), 'Recent developments in the hospital cases', <u>The Modern Law Review</u>, Vol.17, November 1954, pp.547-556

<u>Haley v London Electricity Board</u>, 1965, A.C.788

Hallas, J. (1976), <u>CHCs in Action</u>, Kings Fund, London

Ham, C. (1985), <u>Health Policy in Britain</u> (Second Edition), Macmillan, Basingstoke

Ham, C. (1988), 'Medical negligence claims : the irrestible case for reform', <u>The Independent</u>, 24 January, 1988

Ham, C. Dingwall, R. Fenn, P. and Harris, D. (1988), <u>Medical Negligence: Compensation and Accountability</u>, Kings Fund Institute, London

Harris, N. (1981), Letter to <u>The Times</u>, January 5

<u>Hatcher v Black</u>, 1954, TLR

Hawkins, C. (1985), <u>Mishap or Malpractice?</u> , Blackwell, Oxford

Health Service Commissioner (1976), <u>First Report for the Session 1975-76</u>, HMSO, London

Health Service Commissioner (1979), <u>Annual Report for 1977-78</u>, HCP417, HMSO, London

Health Service Commissioner (1984), <u>Annual Report for 1983-84</u>, HC 537, HMSO, London

Hicks, C. (1987), 'Justice for the few, misery for the many', <u>The Independent</u>, 16 July

<u>Hillyer v St.Bartholomews Hospital</u>, 1909, 2 K.B. 820

<u>Hunter v Harley</u>, 1955, SLT, 213

Jackson, R.M. (1977), <u>The Machinery of Justice in England</u> (Seventh Edition), Cambridge University Press, Cambridge

Jacob, J. (1988), <u>Doctors and Rules : A Sociology of professional values</u>, Routledge, London

Jacob, J. (ed), (1978), <u>Spellers Law Relating to Hospitals</u> (6th edition), H.K.Lewis & Co, London

Jacob, J. and Davies, J.V. (1987), Part 1: Introduction, Sweet and Maxwell's Encyclopedia of Health Services and Medical Law, H.K. Lewis & Co, London

Jones, K (1960), Mental Health and Social Policy, Routledge,Kegan Paul, London

Kennedy, I. (1981), The Unmasking of Medicine, George Allen and Unwin, London

Kennedy, I. (1987) in Byrne, P. (ed), Medicine in Contemporary Society, Kings Fund, London, 1987

Klein, R. (1973), Complaints Against Doctors, Charles Knight, London

Klein, R (1983), Politics of Health, Longman, Harlow

Klein, R. and Shinebourne,A. (1972), 'Doctor's Discipline', New Society, November 16

Klein, R. and Lewis, J. (1976), The Politics of Consumer Representation : a study of Community Health Councils, Centre for Studies in Social Policy, London

Knight, B. (1982), Legal Aspects of Medical Practice, Churchill Livingstone, Edinburgh

Levitt, R. (1976), The Reorganised National Health Service, Croom Helm, London

Levitt, R. (1980), The People's Voice, King Edwards Hospital Fund for London, London

Lim Poh Choo v Camden AHA, 1979, 2 All ER

Little, A. (1977), 'The Race Relations Act, 1976' in Jones, K. Brown, M. and Baldwin, S. (eds), Year Book of Social Policy, 1976, Routledge, Kegan and Paul, London

McLean, S. (1985), 'Accident Compensation Liability Without Fault: the New Zealand perspective', Journal of Social Welfare Law

Marshall v Lindsey County Council, 1935, 1 K.B. 516

Martin, C.R.A. (1973), The Law Relating to Medical Practice, Pitman Medical, London

Martin, C.R.A. (1979), The Law Relating to Medical Practice (Second Edition), Pitman Medical, London

Martin, J.P. (1984), Hospitals in Trouble, Basil Blackwell, London

Mason, J.K. and McCall Smith, R.A. (1983), Law and Medical Ethics, Butterworth, London

Matthews, E.J.T. and Oulton, A.D.M. (1971), Legal Aid and Advice, Butterworth, London

Maynard v West Midlands RHA, 1985, 1 All E.R. 635

MHAC (Mental Health Act Commission), (1985), First Biennial Report of the Mental Health Act Commission, 1983-1985, HMSO, London

MHAC (Mental Health Act Commission), (1987), Second Biennial Report of the Mental Health Act Commission, 1985-1987, HMSO, London

Merrison Report (1975), Report of the Committee of Enquiry into the Regulation of the Medical Profession (Chairman: Dr.A.W.Merrison), HMSO, London

Merrison Report (1979), Royal Commission on the National Health Service (Chairman: Sir Alec Merrison), Cmnd.7615, HMSO, London

Miliband, R (1973), The State in Capitalist Society, Quartet

Books, London

Ministry of Health (1968), <u>The Administrative Structure of Medical and Related Services in England and Wales</u>, HMSO, London

Morris,A and others (1980), <u>Justice for Children</u>, Macmillan, London

<u>Mullins v Parsons</u>, 1971, QB

Murphy, W.T. and Rawlings, R.W. (1981), 'After the Ancien Regime: The Writing of Judgements in the House of Lords 1979/80', <u>Modern Law Review</u>, Vol.44, No.66, November 1981

Murphy, W.T. and Rawlings, R.W. (1982), 'After the Ancien Regime: The Writing of Judgements in the House of Lords 1979/80 Part Two', <u>Modern Law Review</u>, Vol.45, No.1, January 1982

NDG (National Development Group for the Mentally Handicapped), (1976), <u>Mental Handicap : Planning Together</u>, HMSO, London

O'Connell, J. (1975), <u>Ending Insult to Injury: No Fault Insurance for Products and Services</u>, University of Illinois Press, Illinois

Pannick,D, (1988), 'The case for a retrial on compensation', <u>The Guardian</u>, 23 May

Pearson Report (1978), <u>Royal Commission on Civil Liability and Compensation for Personal Injury</u>, Cmnd.7054-1, HMSO, London

Percy, R.A. (1977), <u>Charlesworth on Negligence</u> (Sixth Edition), Sweet and Mazwell, London

Powell, E. (1966), <u>A New Look at Medicine and Politics</u>, Pitman, London

Quam,L, Dingwall,R and Fenn,P (1987), 'Medical Malpractice in Perspective', <u>British Medical Journal</u>, 294, pp.1529-32 and 1597-1600

<u>R v Bateman</u>, 1925, 94 LJKB, 791

<u>Riebl v Hughes</u>, 1980, 114 DLR (3d) 1

Robb, B. (ed), <u>Sans Everything</u>, Nelson, London

Roberts, N. (1967), <u>Mental Health and Mental Illness</u>, Routledge,Kegan and Paul, London

Robinson, J. (1988), <u>A Patient Voice at the GMC – A Lay Member's View of the General Medical Council</u>, Health Rights, London

Robson, W. (1956), <u>Evidence to the Franks Committee</u>

<u>Roe v Ministry of Health</u>, 1954, A.E.R, 13.5.54

Rosenthal, M. (1987), <u>Dealing with Medical Malpractice</u>, Tavistock, London

Savage, W. (1987), 'Important principles at stake', <u>The Guardian</u>, June 3rd

Scott, J.A. (1985), 'Complaints arising from the exercise of clinical judgement', <u>Health Trends</u>, 17, pp.70-72

Secretary of State for Social Services (1986), <u>Primary Health Care: An Agenda for Discussion</u>, Cmnd.9771, HMSO, London

Secretary of State for Social Services (1987), <u>Promoting Better Health – The Government's programme for improving primary health care</u>, Cm.249, HMSO, London

Select Committee on the Parliamentary Commissioner for Administration (1968), <u>Second Report, Session 1967-68</u>, HC 350, HMSO, London

Select Committee on the Parliamentary Commissioner for

Administration (1978), First Report, Session 1977-78, HC 45, HMSO, London

Select Committee on the Parliamentary Commissioner for Administration (1985), Session 1984-85, The Reports of the Health Service Commissioner,1983-84, HMSO, London

Sidaway v Governors of the Bethlem Royal and Maudsley Hospital, 1985, 2 W.L.R., 480

Slack, K. (1977), Social Administration Digest, Journal of Social Policy

Slack, K. (1979), Social Administration Digest, Journal of Social Policy

Smith, Adam (1776), An Inquiry into the Nature and Causes of the Wealth of Nations, Thomas Nelson, Edinburgh

Social Services Committee (1987), First Report on Primary Health Care, January 1987, HC 37, HMSO, London

Society of Labour Lawyers (1978), Legal Services For All, Fabian Society, London

Stacey, F. (1965), 'The machinery for complaints in the National Health Service', Public Administration, Vol.43, 1965, pp.59-70

Stacey, F. (1978), Ombudsmen Compared, Clarendon, Oxford

Street, H. (1968), Justice in the Welfare State, Stevens, London

Timmins, N. (1987), 'How to remove financial insult from injury', The Independent, 17 March

Titmuss, R.M. (1963), Essays on the Welfare State (Second Edition), George Allen and Unwin, London

Titmuss, R.M. (1971), 'Welfare Rights, Law and Discretion', Political Quarterly, 1971

Titmuss, R.M. (1974), Social Policy : An Introduction, George Allen and Unwin, London

US Dept of Health, Education and Welfare (1973), Report of the Secretary's Commission on Medical Malpractice, 18, US Dept of Health, Education and Welfare, Washington, USA

Watkin, B. (1978), The National Health Service: The First Phase, Allen and Unwin, London, 1978

Whiteford v Hunter, 1950, W.N.553

Whitehouse v Jordan, 1980, 1 All E.R.

Wilding, P (1982), Professional Power and Social Welfare, Routledge and Kegan Paul, London

Willcocks, A.J. (1967), The Creation of the National Health Service, Routledge Kegan and Paul, London

Wilsher v Essex AHA, 1988, W.L.R.

Woodhouse Commission (1967), Compensation for Personal Injury in New Zealand, Government Printing Office, Auckland

Wraith, R. and Hutchesson, P. (1973), Administrative Tribunals, George Allen and Unwin, London

Index

Abel-Smith, B vi,55
Aboul Hosn, 29
abortion 36
Administration of
  Justice Act, 15
adultery 36
advertising 36, 37
alcohol abuse 37
Alderson, Baron, 3
Allen, C K, 40
Allen, D, 78
Allsop, J, 7, 59
Apothecaries Society, 13
Area Health Authorities,
  replacement of 44
Ashley-Miller, M vi,vii
Atkin, Lord, 3

'bad practice', 5, 69
balance of probabilities, 24
Bar Council, 71
Barnett v Chelsea and
  Kensington HMC, 23-24, 26
BBC-2 (Horizon), 9
Bell, K, 39, 40, 69
Benson Report, 76
  55-57
Blyth v Birmingham
  Waterworks Co 3

Bolam v Friern Barnet
  HMC, 4, 22, 30
Brahams, D, 79
Brazier, M, 17, 23, 25,
  27, 28, 39, 77, 81
British Medical
Association
  (BMA), 48, 49, 68, 79
British Medical Journal
  (BMJ), 49
Brougham, 71
Brown, R G S, 58
burden of proof, 16

Calman, K C, 8
Campling, J, 44
Canterbury v Spence, 22
Capstick, B, 51, 52
Carson, D, 2, 78
Cartwright Report, 9
Cassidy v Minister of
  Health, 18
Chandler, Raymond, 25, 66
Chandra Battacharya v
  GMC, 37
choice 11
Civil Justice Review, 17,
  25, 26, 27, 28
civil liability, 14
claims consciousness, 26

clinical autonomy, 7, 11
clinical budgeting, 7, 10
clinical judgement, 21, 52,
  55, 57, 63
  error of, 21
Clothier, Sir Cecil, vii
code of duties, 11
code of practice, 61, 64
Cole v Hucks, 17, 83
Common Law, 15
community care, 73
community, costs
  and benefits to, 11, 20,
  21, 28-30, 65-67
Community Health Council
  (CHC), 46, 45, 58-60, 64,
  81, 82
  Association of 46
compensation, 2, 6, 10, 14-17,
  28-31, 34, 42
consent 22-23
Council on Tribunals, 40-44,
  48, 65, 76
compliance 12
complaints about health care,
  1, 2, 13-15, 34, 39-53, 54,
Complaints Investigation
  Procedure, 44
complaints machinery,
  operation of 65
  aims of 70
  approaches, 71-72
confidentiality, 9
consent, 11, 21-23
consultant psychiatrist, 12
consumer representation, 40
consumerism, 9
consumers, 7
contract, 12, 14, 40, 42,
  44, 46
contributory negligence, 26
control system, 10
county courts, 15, 16
Court of Appeal, 15, 16, 18,
  30, 84
courts, the 6, 11, 13-31,
  38, 47, 50, 52-57, 64-67
  access to 26, 27
  adversarial approach 27
  costs, 25, 26, 28
  delays, 25-28
  effectiveness of, 25, 26
  fairness of 25
  inefficiencies of, 25
  inconsistencies of 25,
  27-28

neutrality of, 25
knowledge of, 26
outcomes of, 29-31
proceedings, 25, 47-48,
  66
uncertainties of 25,
  27, 28
welfare role of 6
Crawford v Charing Cross
  Hospital, 20
Crossman, Richard, 8

damage and damages, 17,
  23-25, 29-30
Davies Committee, Report
  on Hospital Complaints,
  46-48, 56, 65, 82
Davis, K C, 6
Denning, Lord, 16, 18-21,
  28, 30, 83
Dennis, I vi
DHSS, 46,47
Dingwall, R, vii, ix, 26,
  29, 77, 79
disciplinary powers, 13,
  14, 32-34
discretionary powers, 6,
  9
District Health
Authorities
  (DHAs), 71
Donaldson, Lord, 30
Donoghue v Stevenson, 3,
  17
Donne, John, 14
Downie, R S, 8
drugs, 36, 37
duty of care, 4, 12, 15-
  24, 26, 30
duty of competence, 12

Eckstien, H 7
Ely Hospital, 47
Ennals, David, 59
Evershed, Lord, 27
Executive Councils (EC),
  64
ethical issues, 8-12, 67
ethical plurality, 11

Fahrni, Dr, 18
Family Practitioner
Committee
  (FPC), 39-46, 54, 59,
  64, 81

Family Practitioners Services
  complaints machinery, 39-46,
  57,68
Farleigh Hospital, 47, 55
Fenn, P. ix, 26, 29, 77, 79
Finch, J, vii,31
Franks Committee, 40, 42
Franklin v Bristol Tramways, 5
Fry,J vii

General Medical Council
  (GMC), ix, 13, 14, 32-39,
  54, 64, 71, 73, 80, 81, 85
GMC Disciplinary Committee, 33
GMC Professional Conduct
  Committee, 33
general practitioner, 7, 12,
  19, 28, 34, 39-46, 47-52
Gerber v Pines, 21
Giesen, D. ix, 4, 17, 18
Gold v Essex County Council,18
good practice, 30, 54, 69
Gostin, L, 6
Green Paper (1968), 42
Griffiths Report, 7
Griffiths, 25
gross neglect in diagnosis 36
The Guardian, 26, 29, 46, 78
Grunfeld ix

Haley v London Electricity
  Board, 27
Ham, C, 7, 28
Harris,D vii,26, 29, 49, 79
Hart, 9
Hatcher v Black
Hawkins, ix
Health Advisory Service (HAS),
  54, 55, 84
health authorities,
  disciplinary powers of, 34,
  46
Health Service Commissioner
  (HSC), 8, 55-60, 64, 81, 84-
  86
Hicks, C, 29
High Court, 15, 16, 26, 27
Hillyer v St. Barts
  Hospital, 17
Hobbes,Thomas, xi
Hospital Complaints Procedure
  Act, 1985, 51
hospital consultants, 7, 18,
  28, 48-50
hospital doctors, 34

hospital services
  complaints
  machinery, 46-53, 68
House of Lords, 15, 16,
  27
Hunter v Harley, 4
Hutchesson, 40

impartiality, 11
informal conciliation and
  mediation, 40, 41, 44,
  45, 64
information,
  given to patient, 21,
  22, 47
Investigating Panels, et
  seq 47
Interluken, 2, 9

Jackson,R.M. 24
Jacob, J, vi, ix, 7, 9,
  12, 18
Jacob,J and Davies,J.V.
  15, 17
Johnson,A vii
Joint Consultants
  Committee, 50
Jones,K. 6
Jowell, J vi
judiciary, neutrality
  of 25
judicial decision-making
  25
judicial welfare, 5-7,
  15, 26, 31

Kennedy, I, 7, 9, 78
Klein, R, ix, 1, 7, 8,
  34, 36, 38, 39, 40, 42,
  47, 58 et seq, 65 et
  seq, 69, 77, 80
Knight, 10
knowledge and
  accessibility, 64

law and welfare, 5-7, 12,
  16
law as welfare, 6, 7
Lawton, Lord, 80
lay involvement, 65
Ledingham,J vii
legal advice, 26
legal aid, 16, 26, 38,
  42, 64, 66
legal proceedings 47, 48
legal services, 7

legally defensive medicine,
30-31
Lehmann,M vi
Levitt, R, 58
Lewis, J, 58 et seq
Lim Poh Choo v Camden AHA,
25, 28, 29
Little, 6
locum, 12
long stay institution, 54
Lord Chancellor, 78
Lord Chief Justice, 78

managerial concerns, 10
market forces, 10
Marshall v Lindsay
County Council, 19
Martin, 5, 15, 19, 28, 29, 3
8, 40, 50, 52, 54
Mason, 8
Maynard v West Midlands RHA
22, 29
MaCall Smith, 8
McLean,S. 79
McNair, J, 3
medical accidents, 2, 26,
54, 69
Medical Act, 1858, 13, 14, 32
Medical Acts, 1950, 1956,
1969, 1978, 1983 et seq
Medical Act, 1978, 33
medical care, standard of 13
medical ethics, 10
medical knowledge, 20
medical negligence, 1-9, 12-
32, 34, 39, 55, 64, 66, 67,
69
definitions of 3-5
medical profession, 7
Medical Protection Society,
27, 28
medical treatment, 63
Mental Health Act, 1982, 61
Mental Health Act, 1983, 61
Mental Health Act, 1959
Mental Health Act
Commission 61 et seq
Merrison, 8, 33, 34, 38, 42,
81
Merrison Commission, 80, 82
Merrison Report, 33, 59, et
seq
Miliband, R, 25
Milton, John, 68
Miracle at Morgans Creek, 14

monetary loss
and compensation, 17,
29
Morris,A. 6
Mullins v Parsons, 21
Murphy, 25, 27

National Development
Group for Mentally
Handicapped, 61
National Health
Insurance, 13
National Health Service
(NHS), 32, 39-53, 56
Act 1946, 32
complaints machinery
39-53, 55-60, 62-64
Reorganization Act,
1973, 56
natural justice, 36
National Insurance Act,
1911, 32
negligence, 2-5, 12, 15-
32, 39, 55, 64
definitions of 3-5
New Zealand, 9, 79, 81
no-fault approach, 67, 68
non-monetary loss
and compensation, 17,
29
nurses, 18
Nuffield Provincial
Hospitals Trust, vi,vii

O'Connell,J. 27-29
Observer, The, 9
ombudsman 55-57

Pannick,D. 26
Parliamentary
Commissioner
for Administration, 49,
55, 56
House of Commons
Committee for 26, 49
Patients First, 43, 44
patients friend, 58,
59, 66
patients grievances, 13
Pearson Commission, 15,
16, 79, 81
Percy, 4, 17, 19
Pharmaceutical Society,
34
Powell, Enoch, 8
Prentice,D vii

pressure groups, 7
primary health care 44-45
priorities, 7, 8
professional autonomy, 8, 10,
  11
professional care, 63
professional duty, 6, 10, 12,
  17
professional misconduct, 34-39
professional negligence, 3,
  12, 15-16, 55
professional power
  and status, 7, 8, 17, 51
professional self-regulation,
  9, 10, 13, 32-39
professional standards, 2, 4,
  5, 8, 12, 13, 20, 32, 33, 55
professionalism, 7, 8
professional/lay relationship,
  9

quality of care, 14
Quam,L. ix, 77

R v Bateman, 4
Rawlings,R.W. 25, 27
reasonable care, 30
redress, 7, 13
reforms, proposals for 75-87
  general reforms 75-78
  specific reforms 78-81
  our proposals 82-87
research, 9
resource allocation, 7-11
Regional Health
  Authorities (RHAs), 71
Regional Medical Officer, 47
  et seq
remedy at law, 56
Review Body on Civil Justice,
  26
Riebl v Hughes, 22
right to assistance, 64
right to complain, 6, 64
right to know, 6
right to welfare, 6
rights, individual, 6, 28
rights, service-users, 6
risks, in medical practice,
  19-22
Robb, B, 55
Roberts, N, 6
Robinson, J, 34, 38, 39, 65
Robson, W, 40
Roe v Ministry of Health, 19,
  20

Rosenthal, ix, 67, 79, 81
Royal College of
  Physicians, 13
Royal College of
  Surgeons, 13
Royal Commission of
  Legal Services, 76

Saatchi and Saatchi, 78
Savage, 38
Scarman, Lord, 22, 25, 29
Scott, 46, 50, 51
Scottish Mental Welfare
  Commission, 62
Secretary of State
  for Social Services,
  39, 41, 43-48
Shakespeare, William, 24
Shaw, George Bernard, 10
Sidaway v Governors of
  the Bethlem Royal and
  Maudsley Hospital, 22,
  29
Shinebourne,A. 34, 38
Slack,K. 43, 49, 60
Smith, Adam, 10
social security for
  physically disabled
  people, 2
Social Administration
  Association, vi, vii
Social Science
  Research Council vi,vii
Social Services
  Committee, 45
Society of Labour
  Lawyers, 45
Stacey, ix, 55-58
standards of care, 3-5,
  12, 5, 61
standards of proof, 16,
  39
'submerged iceberg' of
  complaints and
  litigation, 1, 8, 66
Street,H. 67
surrogate carer, 12
Sweden, 67, 79, 81
Thomas, Mrs Evelyn, 9
Times Law Report, The, 29
Timmins, N, 28
Titmuss, R M, 6
torts, 14-24, 65, 67
Treasury, The, 74
trust, 9, 10

UKCC 73
US Department of Health,
  Education and Welfare, 30
USA, 67
vicarious liability, 17-19
voluntary hospitals, 19

Wall,J vii
Watkin, B, 48
welfare law, 5-7
White Paper,
  Improving Primary Health
Care, 45
White Paper,
  NHS Reorganization, 42
White Paper, 1987, 65
Whiteford v Hunter, 19
Whiteford v Jordan, 73
Whiteford v Jordan, 20-21,
  25, 26, 30, 79
Whittingham Hospital, 47
Willcocks,A. 7
Williams, Sir Edgar, vii
Williams, Shirley, 58
Wilsher v Essex AHA, 16, 26
Woodhouse Commission (New
  Zealand)
Wraith, 40